A MUSSALMANI BENGALI-ENGLISH DICTIONARY

A MUSSALMANI BENGALI-ENGLISH DICTIONARY

by

The Rev. WILLIAM GOLDSACK

Introduction by : Sila Basak

GYAN PUBLISHING HOUSE
NEW DELHI-110002

A Mussalmani Bengali-English Dictionary

ISBN: 81-212-0942-0

Rs. 340

Published in 2007 in India by
Gyan Publishing House
5, Ansari Road, Daryaganj, New Delhi-110002
Phones : 23261060, 23282060, Fax : 91-011-23285914
E-mail : books@gyanbooks.com
Website : http://www.gyanbooks.com

Laser Typesetting at: Master Computers, Delhi
Printed at: Salasar Imaging System, Delhi

PREFACE

Mussalmani Bengali is the name given to that form of the Bengali language which is used by the Muhammadans of Bengal. It takes its name from the large admixture of Arabic and Persian terms to be found therein, and which were introduced into the language by the Mussalman conquerors of Bengal in the twelfth century. Its importance may be gauged by the fact that the Bible Society finds it necessary to publish the Christian Scriptures in this dialect for the exclusive use of Muslims : whilst hundreds of books and papers are published by Muhammadans themselves in the same dialect.

The Muhammadan supremacy in Bengal, before the advent of British rule, imposed an almost exclusively Persi-Arabic vocabulary upon the people wherever matters affecting the administration of the country were concerned. This 'Mussalmani' vocabulary still persists, and in all legal and zemindari documents finds expression in numerous words of Muslim origin.

Again in the everyday speech of the Muhammadan masses Mussalmani Bengali is the common medium of intercourse, and hundreds of Arabic and Persian words are constantly being used which have no connection whatever with pure Bengali, and which find no place in any ordinary dictionary of the Bengali language.

So far the writer is aware, no attempt has hitherto been made to compile a dictionary of these foreign terms, and although many of them are to be found scattered through the pages of ordinary Bengali dictionaries, there are still hundreds of words in use to-day for the meaning of which the reader will search in vain the pages of any existing dictionary. The following pages represent an attempt to supply a list of Mussalmani Bengali words, which, though not exhaustive, will, it is hoped, be found to contain most of the words of Arabic and Persian origin in common use by the Muhammadans of Bengal. This list should be found useful by missionaries, planters, Government officials, and all who came into contact either with the literature or the spoken language of the Muslims of this Province.

One initial difficulty which presented itself the moment such a compilation was suggested was the complete absence of any authoritative standard of transliteration of the letters of the Persi-Arabic alphabet into Bengali characters. A reference to current Mussalmani Bengali literature and to the standard dictionaries of the Bengali language, when such words are found, reveals the widest discrepancy in the spelling of these words. Thus, for example, the well-known Arabic word مُخْتَار *mukhtar*, is represented by the author of the well-known 'Prakritibad' by the word মোক্তার : S. C. Mitra, in his comprehensive 'Student's Dictionary' writes the word মুক্তিয়ার, whilst Houghton correctly renders it মুখ্‌তার. This diversity in the transliteration of Arabic and Persian letters is, to some extent, due to the presence in the Persi-Arabic alphabet of a number of letters which have no counterpart in the Bengali alphabet : hence writers have been left to find their own substitutes.

The attempt to invent Bengali letters or diacritical signs to represent these additional letters does not commend itself to the author. It has been done in English by the Royal Asiatic Society, but the result is meaningless to all who are not acquainted with the Arabic and Persian scripts. After mature consideration, therefore, it has seemed better to adopt some consistent and scientific standard of transliteration for letters common to both the Persi-Arabic and Bengali alphabets, and to render the remainder phonetically by means of the existing Bengali alphabet. Any such method of transliteration, however, must inevitably come into conflict with spellings which have by common use become fixed in Bengali. In such cases the current spelling has been generally accepted, even at the cost of scientific accuracy. Hence such spellings as হারাম, হালাল, তামাক and many others, have been allowed to stand, notwithstanding the absence of the long vowel in the first syllable in the original word. Where 'Mussalmani' words are at present rendered in different conficting ways in current Bengali literature, an attempt has been made to give a correct transliteration, though here, as always, the troublesome letters referred to above cause endless difficulty

Of all the letters peculiar to the Persi-Arabic alphabet the letter ع '*ain*' is the most troublesome. The Bengali alphabet has no corresponding letter, nor has the Bengali language any corresponding sound. In Arabic the pronounciation of this letter largely depends upon its accompanying vowel, and we have, generally speaking, followed the same practice when representing it in Bengali characters. Thus in the word عِلْم *'ilm* 'ain would be represented by ই, whilst in the word عُمر *'umr* its Bengali equivalent would be উ, and in the word عَمَل *'amal* it is অ. The Royal Asiatic Society, it may be mentioned, represents this letter by the *spiritus lenis*'.

Another Arabic letter which calls for notice is the letter ه, h, which when written at the end of a word, is frequently written with two dots above, and then pronounced as t. It then becomes a *servile* letter, and it seems better, in every way, to transliterate the letter according to its sound rather than in strict relation to its original form. Hence the word قيامة *quiyamah* is so well-known and pronounced as কিয়ামৎ that it would seem an impertinence to write it otherwise.

The letter ث is properly pronounced as th and should, therefore, be represented in Bengali by থ. Usage, however, has almost universally represented it by স, as may be seen in the familiar words হদীস, সবুৎ, and ওয়ারিস. We have, therefore, adopted this form when transliterating the letter into Bengali.

The absence of any w in the Bengali language has made the adoption of any satisfactory substitute for the Persi-Arabic و *waw*, a matter of great difficulty. This is added to by the spellings, now more or less fixed, which have been adopted for various words containing this letter. Thus the words উকীল, ওকালৎ and বিদাৎ, have each represented و *waw* by a different Bengali letter. These spellings have become fixed, and it would be presumptious to alter them in accordance with any mechanical theory of transliteration, however desirable in itself.

The Arabic letter غ should properly be represented in Bengali by the letter ঘ, but custom has almost invariably chosen to dispense with the aspirate any use গ instead. This usage has now become universal, so that the spelling of words like গজব anger, গফর forgiveness, গরজ desire, গরীব poor, and many others have become fixed. In such cases we have retained the customary spelling.

For the rest, it need only be remarked that the learned Dr. Fallon in his monumental Hindustani-English Dictionary was obliged to represent no less than six letters of the Persi-Arabic alphabet by the English *z* and the Deb Nagri अ. This remark well serves to illustrate the difficulty which faces the orthographer who attempts to render Persian and Arabic words by Bengali characters.

It only remains to add that in this dictionary those words which carry the same, or nearly the same, idea have been separated by a comma, whilst words conveying a different meaning have been separated by a semicolon. In cases where the correct spelling is adopted in the text, other spellings to be found in current literature are often given within brackets Conversely where the popular spelling has been followed, the correct spelling has generally been given within brackets. In each case the practice which has been followed has been made clear.

With one or two exceptions, the original sources of the words brought together in this dictionary have been indicated by Roman capitals. The list of abbreviations given below, will indicate to what languages these refer. The letters in Italics refer to the parts of speech, and, like the Roman capitals, have been placed immediately after the words themselves.

The sub-joined table will indicate the method of transliteration which has been followed, with the exceptions mentioned above, in the following pages.

W. G.

INTRODUCTION

The term Musalman Bengali was, perhaps, first employed by the Reverend James Long in his *A Catalogue of Bengali Works* (Kolkata, 1855). In his view, '...the Musalmans have formed in Bengali a lingua franca, a mixture of Bengali and Urdu, called the boatman's language. This must eventually give way to the overwhelming influence of the Bengali.' If this was a kind patois current only among the boatmen, the use of such epithet to denote the language of a community was hardly justified. The Reverend was, however, armed with a body of writings, which he called Musalman-Bengali literature, whose vocabulary had a preponderance of Perso-Arabic elements. This was an artificial literary style, in vogue between the mid-eighteenth century and the early twentieth, quite distinct from the general trend to which the Muslim poets also contributed. Professor Suniti Kumar Chatterji estimates that there are 4.55% foreign words in Bengali of which Persian (and that includes Arabic, Turkish and Hindi or Urdu words imported mostly through Persian) elements account for 3.30%. He adds that the colloquial used in a Bengali household would normally have 8% such elements while the body of literature mentioned above includes as high as 32%. Such works were mostly translations or adaptations of Persian or Hindusthani (as it was then known) tales and issued initially in cheap editions from printing presses in north Kolkata — and later from Dhaka — in the format of Arabic, Persian Urdu books – the pagination ran from right to left. These became quite popular among semi-literate Muslim readers first in towns, and later in villages too. The popularity of such texts also made inroads elsewhere. The Reverend Long informed us that, 'The Bible society have printed the Gospel of Luke in this dialect, and are proceeding with other portions of the Scriptures.'

Since the Reverend Long gave the name Musalmani Bengali, other cataloguers like J. F. Blumhardt and scholars like Dr Dinesh Chandra Sen, Professor Suniti Kumar Chatterji and Professor Sukumar Sen have used the same or its slight variations in denoting this peculiar form. The

Reverened William Goldsack seems to have followed this tradition. In the Preface of his book, he explains :

> Mussalmani Bengali is the name given to that form of the Bengali language which is used by the Muhammedans of Bengal. It takes its name from the large admixture of Arabic and Persian terms to be found therein, and which were introduced into the language by the Mussalman conquerors of Bengal in the twelfth century. Its importance may be gauged by the fact that the Bible Society finds it necessary to publish the Christian Scriptures in this dialect for exclusive use of Muslims; whilst hundreds of books and papers are published by Muhammadans themselves in the same dialect. ...
>
> Again in the everyday speech of the Muhammadan masses Musalmani Bengal is the common medium of intercourse, and hundreds of Arabic and Persian words are constantly being used which have no connection whatever with pure Bengali, and which find no place in any ordinary dictionary of the Bengali language.

This notion of purity ran through most of the leading writers of Bengali since the days of William Carey and it took time to get rid of this.

It goes to the credit of the Reverend Goldsack that he proceeded to compile such Arabic, Persian, Turkish and Hindi words which were in common use among the Muslims of Bengal though he considered these extraneous to the language. His claim that his is the first attempt to compile a dictionary of these foreign terms is accurate. He gives us nearly 6000 such words indicating the language from which a particular word is taken and also showing its grammatical category. Some repetitions will be found in that he has included both the noun and its verb (by adding Bengali verb) form. For example, we have *jawāb* (a reply, noun), followed by *jawāb karā* (to reply), and *pasanda* (choice, noun), followed by *pasanda kara* (to choose). Still it will be regarded as a much valued pioneering work. Unfortunately, the date of the publication of *A Mussalmani Bengali–English Dictionary* is not given in the reprint of the work (Dhaka, 1970), but we gather that this appeared in 1923. Two other such dictionaries have appeared since then : *Perso-Arabic Elements in Bengali* by Ghulam Maqsud Hilali (Dhaka, 1967) and *Bangla Sahitye Arbi-Farsi Shabda* by Harendra Chandra Pal (Dhaka, 1967). Despite their other merits, these two have not surpassed Goldsack's work in the number of entries listed.

The present edition is a photographic reproduction. We are sure that a valuable contribution such as this will be of immense use to scholars and ordinary readers. I would like to thank the Gyan Publishing House, New Delhi, for undertaking the publication of this valuable book. I also like to take this opportunity to express my love for my two grandsons, Subheccha (Prince) and Rebanta (Raj) whose presence inspired me to take up this project.

First Published 1923
January, 2007
Kolkata 700031

Sila Basak

LIST OF ABBREVIATIONS

A.	stands for	Arabic.		*V.*	" "	Verb.
P.	" "	Persian.		*Pro.*	" "	Pronoun.
H.	" "	Hindi.		*Sing.*	" "	Singular.
T.	" "	Turkish.		*Plu.*	" "	Plural.
N.	" "	Noun.		*Comp.*	" "	Compounds.
Adj.	" "	Adjective.		*Esp.*	" "	Especially
Adv.	" "	Adverb.		c.f.	" "	Compare.
Con.	" "	Conjunction.		i.e.	" "	That is.
Prep.	" "	Preposition.		*Corr.*	" "	Corruption.
Int.	" "	Interjection.				

THE PERSI-ARABIC ALPHABET AS EXPRESSED IN BENGALI CHARACTERS

The Vowels and Diphthongs

آ	اِ	اِي	اُ	اُو	اِي	اَي	اَو	اَو
আ	ই	ঈ	উ	ঊ	এ	ঐ	ও	ঔ

The Consonants

ب	پ	ت	ٹ	ث	ج	چ	ح	خ
ব	প	ত	ট	স	জ	চ and ছ	হ	খ
د	ڈ	ذ	ر	ڑ	ز	س	ش	ص
দ	ড	জ	র	ড়	জ	স	শ	স
ض	ط	ظ	ع	غ	ف	ق	ك	گ
জ	ত	জ	various	ঘ	ফ	ক	ক	গ
ل	م	ن	و	ه	ي	ء		
ল	ম	ন	various	হ	various	অ		

MUSSALMANI BENGALI-ENGLISH

DICTIONARY.

অ

অকফ—*See* ওকফ.

অকদ, A. *n.* A knot ; a contract, an agreement.

অকদনামা, A. *n.* A written contract, a marriage settlement.

অকল, A. *n.* Understanding, wisdom, intellect. (Often corruptly written আকেল).

অকলমন্দ, A. *adj.* Wise, intelligent.

অকু—*See* ওকু.

অকুয়াৎ—*See* ওকুয়াৎ.

অকুফ—*See* ওকুফ.

অচানক, H. *adv.* Unwillingly ; suddenly ; unconsciously.

অছিলা—*See* ওসীলা.

অজু—*See* ওজু

অজুহাৎ—*See* ওজুহাৎ.

অতর, A. *n.* Otto of roses, essence.

অতরদান, A. *n.* A smelling-bottle ; perfume.

অত্তার, A. *n.* A perfumer, a druggist.

অদল, A. *n.* Justice, equity.

অদলবদল, A. *n.* Change, exchange.

অদল করা, A. *v.* To do justice, to judge.

অদুল, A. *n.* Disobedience, violation, infraction.

অদুল করা, A. *v.* To disobey, to break (a law).

অন্দর, P. *adv.* Within, inside. *adj.* Inner.

অমর—*See* উমর.

অম্বর, A. *n.* A perfume (*ambergris*) ; cotton.

অরক, A. *n.* Juice, sap ; perspiration ; spirits.

অরগজা, H. *n.* A yellow perfume.

অরফ. A. *adv.* Otherwise called; *alias.*

অরফে, A. *adv.* Same as অরফ.

অল্‌বত্তা, A. *adv.* Certainly, surely.

অলাকা—*See* এলাকা.

অলি—*See* ওলী.

অলুফা, A. *n.* A pension, a salary; subsistence money.

অসা, A. *n.* A rod, a staff, a sceptre.

অসাবরদার, A. *n.* One who carries a sceptre or staff.

অসী—*See* ওসী.

অহদ, A. *n.* A compact, a promise, an agreement.

অহদনামা, A. *n.* A written agreement; a will.

আ

A. *n.* A law, an edict: a constitution, a code.

দেওয়ানী আইন, Civil law.

ফৌজদারী আইন, Criminal law.

আইনমত, A. *adv.* According to law

আইন কানুন, A. *n.* Laws and regulations.

আইনা—*See* আয়না.

আইন্দা—*See* আয়েন্দা.

আইব—*See* আয়েব.

আইয়াম, A. *n.* Days; time; season.

আইশ, A. *n.* Happiness, delight.

আউওল, A. *adj.* First, best; (land) which produces a sixteen anna crop.

আওজ, A. *n.* A change, a substitute: a reward.

আওজে, A. *adv.* Instead of.

আওটান, H. *v.* To turn round, to stir round.

আওবাশ, A. *n.* A profligate, debauchee.

আওয়াজ, P. *n.* A sound, a noise, a report; voice, cry.

আওয়ারা, P. *n.* A wandering: a vagabond.

আওরঙ্গ, P. *n.* A throne, a crown

আওরৎ—*See* ঔরৎ.

আওলাৎ—*See* আলাৎ.

আওলাদ, A. *n.* Sons progeny; tribe, race. (*Plu.* of ওলদ. but often incorrectly used as a *sing*).

আওলিয়া, A. *n.* In law 'the nearest of kin'; companions, friends; Muslim saints.

আওসৎ, A. *adj.* Middle, average, subordinate. *n.* A sub-lease.

আওহাল, A. *n.* Conditions, circumstances. (A corruption of আহ্‌ওয়াল.)

আওসাফ, A. *n.* Attributes, qualities; [a description.

আকৃবৎ—*See* আকিবৎ.

আক্‌বর, A. *adj.* Greater, more illustrious, more important.

আল্লাহ আকবর 'God is most great'.

আকদ, A. *n.* A marriage portion, a dower.

আক্‌রা, H. *adj.* Dear, costlv.

আক্‌রাম, A. *n.* Favours, honours.

আক্‌সর, A. *adj.* Many, most, much. *adv.* Generally, frequently.

আক্‌সাৎ. A *n.* Instalments. (*Plu.* of কিস্ত.)

আক্‌সাম, A. *n.* Kinds, sorts.

আকায়েদ, A. *n.* Religious beliefs; articles of a creed.

আকিবৎ, A. *n.* Futurity; end, conclusion. (Also written আকবৎ.)

আকিবৎ আন্দেশ, A. *adj.* Discreet far-sighted.

আকীক, A. *n.* A cornelian.

আকীকা, A. *n.* A Muhammadan ceremony performed six days after the birth of a child. It consists in shaving the child's head and offering a sacrifice.

আকীদা, A. *n.* Religious belief or creed; a profession of faith.

আকেল, (A অকল). *n.* Wisdom, understanding.

আকেলমন্দ, A. *adj.* Reasonable, wise, intelligent.

আখজ, A. *n.* Objection, hostility, malice, enmity; a taking, a seizing.

আখ্তা, A *n.* A castrated animal, a gelding.

আখ্তা করা, A. *v.* To castrate.

আখ্বার, A. *n.* News; newspapers. (*Plu.* of খবর).

আখ্রোট, H. *n.* A walnut.

আখের, A. *n.* The end; the future.

আখেরী, A. *adj.* Final, terminal; future.

আখেরৎ, A. *n.* The next world, the future life.

আখ্নূন, P. *n.* A teacher, an instructor. [land.

আগত রাইয়তী জমী, A. *n.* Subrented

আগত খামার জমী, A. *n.* Land rented direct from the zemindar.

আগ্বান হওয়া, A. *v.* To go forward, to advance.

আগা, T. *n.* A Moghul; a title of honour.

আগাজ, P. *n.* Beginning, commencement.

আগিলা, H. *adj.* Coming, next; preceding, former.

আঙ্গুর, P. *n.* The grape.

আঙ্গুর-রস, P. *n.* Wine.

আঙ্গশতরী, P. *n.* A ring.

আচকান, P. *n.* A kind of long coat worn by servants.

আচার, P. *n.* Pickles.

আজ্গবী, H. *adj.* Unexpected, sudden; strange. *adv.* Unexpectedly; suddenly.

আজ্দাদ, A. *n.* Ancestors.

আজ্নবী, A. *n.* A foreigner, a stranger. *adj.* Strange, new, foreign. [species.

আজ্নাস, A. *n.* Goods; kinds,

আজব, A. *adj.* Strange, wonderful.

আজব-ঘর, A. *n.* A museum.

আজ্বক—*See* উজবক.

আজব তামাশা, A. *n.* A show, an exhibition, a surprising sight.

আজমৎ, A. *n.* Greatness, magnificence.

আজ্মান, A. *n.* Times, seasons.

আজমায়েশ, P. *n.* Trial, temptation; experiment.

আজর, A. *n.* Remuneration, reward.

আজল, A. *n.* A beginning, a fixed period.

রোজ-আজল, The day of one's birth when his destiny is registered.

আজ্লাফ, A. *n.* The lower classes, base-born people.

আজ্‌হা, A. *n.* Sacrifice.
ঈদ্‌-উল্‌-আজ্‌হা. the Muhammadan 'Feast of Sacrifice.'

আজাজীল, A. *n.* A fallen angel of that name.

আজাদ, A. *adj.* Free, discharged. *n.* A freedman.

আজাদ করা, A. *v.* To release, to set free ; to dismiss.

আজাদী, A. *n.* Freedom.

আজান, A. *n.* The summons to Muhammadan prayer. *Azan.*

আজান দেওয়া, A. *v.* To sound the call to Muslim prayers.

আজাব, A. *n.* Punishment, vengeance, torment.

আজায়েব, A. *n.* Wonders.

আজার, A. *n.* Sickness, trouble ; pain.

আজার দেওয়া, A. *v.* To trouble to vex, to injure ; to persecute.

আজারবন্দ, A. *adj.* Afflicted with trouble or sickness.

আজারী, A. *adj.* Sick, diseased.

আজীজ, A. *adj.* Dear, beloved ; respected. *n.* Friend, a relative.

আজীব, A. *adj.* Unique. wonderful.

আজীম, A. *adj.* Great, important.

আজীম করা, A. *v.* To exalt, to respect.

আজীর, P. *adj.* Poor, helpless. *n.* A hired labourer ; a slave.

আজ্‌রদার, A. *n.* A hired labourer.

আজ্‌রদারী, A. *n.* Hire, payment ; piece-work.

আজ্‌রা, A. *n.* Hire, wages, reward. (A corruption of আজর).

আজেজ, A. *adj.* Weak, incapable ; frustrated.

আঞ্জাম, P. *n.* End, result, completion ; arrangement and supply.

আঞ্জাম করা, P. *v.* To conduct, to manage ; to comply with ; to finish.

আঞ্জীর, P. *n.* A fig.

আঞ্জুমান, P. *n.* A society, an institution, a committee ; an assembly.

আড়ৎ, H. *n.* Commission, brokerage, agency ; place of business.

আড়ৎদার, H. *n.* A commission-agent, a broker.

আণ্ডা, H. *n.* An egg.

আতর—*See* অতর.

আৎরাফ, A. *n.* Limits, boundaries. (*Plu.* of তরফ).

আতলস, A. *n.* Satin.

আতশ, P. *n.* Fire ; anger ; a wicked person.

আতশবাজী, P. *n.* Fireworks.

আতশী, P. *adj.* Fiery

আতা, A. *n.* A gift.

আতাই, P. *n.* Amateur musicians.

আদ—*See* আদু.

আদৎ, A. *n.* A custom, a habit. *adj.* Whole, complete.

আদতে, A. *adv.* By custom, habitually ; on the whole.

আদদ্‌, A. *n.* Number, computation ; time, turn.

আদ্‌না, A. *adj.* Low, base, inferior, common.
n. The common people.

আদব—*See* আদাব.

আদম, A. *n.* Loss, lack of, cessation ; Adam.

আদম সুমারী, A. *n.* A census.

আদমী, A. *n.* A man, a human being.

আদমীয়ৎ, A. *n.* Humanity; sympathy.

আদল—*See* অদল.

আদা, A. *n.* Performance, payment, fulfilment of an agreement; perfection.

আদা করা, A. *v.* To execute, to perform, to carry out; to repay.

আদা মালগুজারী, A. *n.* Payment of revenue.

আদাওয়ৎ, A. *n.* Enmity, hatred.

আদাব, A. *n.* A salutation; good manners, politeness.

Int. 'Your humble servant!' 'Good day' (Inferior to superior.)

আদাব করা. A. *v.* To salute.

আদাব কায়েদা, A. *n.* Rules, etiquette.

আদাবিদ, A. *n.* Payment of a debt.

আদায়, A. *n.* A collecting, a receiving, collection, realization.

আদায় করা, A. *v.* To collect, to realize.

আদায়-পত্র, A. *n.* A realization of debts; a written contract.

আদালৎ, (A অদালৎ). *n.* A court of justice, a tribunal.

দেওয়ানী আদালৎ, A civil court.

ফৌজ্‌দারী আদালৎ, A criminal court.

আদালৎ করা, A *v.* To administer justice, to try suits at law.

আদালতী, A. *adj.* Judicial, relating to the courts.

আদেল, A. *adj.* Just, equitable.

আন্, P. A plural suffix, as ওয়ারিসান heirs.

আন্‌ওয়ার, A. *n.* Lights.

আন্‌সার, A. *n.* Helpers. A special title given to those inhabitants of Madina who *helped* Muhammad on the occasion of his flight thither.

আনার, P. *n.* A pomegranate.

আন্দাজ, P. *n.* A guess, a conjecture; valuation, estimate.

আন্দাজী, P. *adj.* Conjectural.

আন্দাম, P. *n.* The body; form, stature.

আন্দেশা, P. *n.* Thought, meditation, care; doubt, suspicion.

আপস্, H. *pro.* Each other, one another; mutual.

আপোস, H. *n.* A compromise.

আপোস করা, H. *v.* To settle, to compromise.

আফ্‌ওয়াহ, A. *n.* Rumours, news.

আফজুদ, P. *adv.* More, abundantly. *n.* Increase.

আফৎ, A. *n.* Misfortune, calamity, disaster, misery.

আফৎ পড়া, A. *v.* To be overtaken by a calamity.

আফ্‌তাব, P. *n.* The sun.

আফ্‌তাবা—*See* আবতাবা.

আফ্‌রা, P. *n.* An insect blight which attacks growing rice.

আফ্‌শান, P. *n.* A sprinkling, a scattering, a shaking (of the hands in anger).

আফ্‌শানী কাগজ, P. *n.* A letter studded with gold leaf.

আফ্‌সানা, P. *n.* A fable, a romance.

আফ্‌সানী করা, P. *v.* To romance.

আফ্‌সোস, P. *n.* Regret; lament, sorrow.

আফসোস করা, P. *v.* To regret.

আফীম, A. *n.* Opium.

আফু, A. *n.* Pardon, remission.

আব, P. *n.* Water.

আব হাওয়া, P. *n.* Climate.

আব্ওয়াব্, A. *n.* Chapters; doors; extra demands, in addition to rent, made by zemindars from their tenants. (*Plu.* of বাব).

আব্কার, P. *n.* A seller or distiller of wine or spirits; a wine merchant.

আবকারী, P. *n.* The business of a distiller; a duty levied on distilleries; excise.

আব্কারী দারোগা, P. *n.* An excise inspector.

আব্কারী মহল, P. *n.* An excise department.

আবখোরা, P. *n.* A drinking vessel, a goblet.

আব্ছায়া, P. *n.* Light reflected on the surface of water, and hence অপচ্ছায়া, an apparition.

আবতর, A. *adj.* Ruined, spoiled, worthless, disorderly; false.

আবতরী, A. *n.* Depravity, worthlessness.

আবতাবা, P. *n.* A water-pot, a kettle.

আবদার, P. *n.* A whim, a strongly expressed wish; solicitation. One who indulges in whims. A servant who prepares water for domestic purposes. *adj.* Brilliant, polished; pure.

আবদারী, P. *n.* Brilliance; purity.

আব্দীদা. P. *adj.* In tears.

আব্দাল, P. *n.* A hermit, a saint.

আব্নুস, A. *n.* Ebony.

আবরওয়ান, P. *n.* Running water.

আবরঙ্গ, P. *n.* A throne, an ornamental chair.

আবরা, P. *n.* The outer cloth of a lined garment. (*See* আস্তর).

আবরূ, P. *n.* Dignity, honour, reputation.

আবলাৎ *See* আলাৎ.

আবাদ, P. *adj.* Inhabited, cultivated, prosperous. *n.* In *compounds* a city, as Allahabad.

আবাদ করা, P. *v.* To cultivate; to make a place habitable.

আবাদী, P. *adj.* Arable, fit for cultivation.

আবাদ বেশী, P. *n.* First assessment of cultivated lands.

আবু, A. *n.* A father.

আবেদ, A. *n.* A worshipper, a devotee.

আব্দ, A. *n.* A slave, a servant.

আম, A. *adj.* Common, general, public. (Opposite of খাস special, particular.)

আমওয়াল A. *n.* Goods, wealth, property. (*Plu.* of মাল).

আমদ, P. *n.* Coming, arrival.

আমদরফৎ, P. *n.* A coming and going; imports and exports.

আমদা, (A. আমাদা). Ready, prepared.

আমদানী, A. *n.* Imports; income, receipts, rents, revenue.

আমদানী হুমার, A. *n.* Total receipts.

আম-মুখ্‌তার, A. *n.* One given general powers to act in legal matters ; an agent, an attorney.

আম-মুখ্‌তারনামা, A. *n.* A written power of attorney ; an order giving possession of property.

আমল, (A. অমল) *n.* Work, business, act ; a district ; administration ; the period of a ruler's government. [sion.

আমল দেওয়া, A. *v.* To give possession.

আমলদার, A. *n.* A ruler ; an agent, a tax-collector.

আমলদারী, A. *n.* Rule, administration ; collection of revenue.

আমলনামা, A. *n.* A letter or document authorising one to administer some office, or take possession of property.

আমলে আনা, A. *v.* To perform.

আমলদস্তক A. *n.* A written order giving possession ; a warrant, a writ.

আমল পত্তি, H. *n.* A hem.

আমলা, A. *n.* An officer, an agent ; a tax-collector. (*Plu.* of আমেল, but commonly used as a *sing.*)

আমলী, A. *adj.* Practical. *n.* Payment in kind. [peace.

আমান, A. *n.* Safety, protection ;

আমানৎ, A. *n.* A deposit ; care, trust ; safety, protection.

adj. Deposited, entrusted to.

আমানৎ রাখা, A. *v.* To deposit.

আমানৎকারী, A. *n.* Depositor.

আমানৎদার, A. *n.* A custodian, a guardian.

আমানৎদারী, A. *n.* Guardianship, trust.

আমানতী, A. *adj.* Deposited.

আমানৎনামা, A. *n.* A deed of trust.

আমীজ, P. *n.* A mixture ; a shade. *adj.* Mixed.

আমীন, A. *n.* A commissioner, a trustee ; a surveyor ; a judge. *adj.* Faithful.

Int. Amen, so be it .

আমীনী, A. *n.* The office of an *amin.* Custody, guardianship.

আমীর, A. *n.* A prince, a ruler. An *Amir.*

আমীর-উল্‌-মোমেনীন, 'The Prince of the Believers' : a title of the Muslim Khalifs.

আমীরজাদা, A. *n.* A prince.

আমীরাণা, A. *n.* Nobility, greatness. *adj.* Noble, great.

আমীরী, A. *n.* Nobility.

আমুল মামুল, A. *adv.* According to custom.

আমূ, A. *n.* A paternal uncle.

আমেজ—*See* আমীজ.

আমেল, A. *n.* An officer of Government, a collector of revenue.

আমেলদার, A. *n.* A collector of revenue.

আম্বিয়া A. *n.* Prophets. (*Plu.* of নবী.)

আম্মা, H. *n.* A mother.

আয়না, P. *n.* A mirror, a looking-glass.

আয়েশ, A. *n.* Luxury, enjoyment.

আয়ুব, A. *n.* Job.

আয়েৎ, A. *n.* A sign; a verse of the Quran.

আয়মা, A. *n.* A grant of land rent free. or at a low rental, as a reward.

আয়মাদার, A. *n.* One to whom rent-free land is granted as a reward.

আয়াম, A. *n.* Days; time, period.

আয়েন্দা, P. *adv.* Future, coming; *adv.* In future.

আয়েব, A. *n.* Vice, imperfection, fault. বে-আয়েব. Sinless, faultless.

আয়েসা, H. *adv.* Like, such.

আরওয়াহ্, A. *n.* Spirits, souls.

আরক, (A. অরক) *n.* Liquor, spirits; sap, essence.

আরকান A. *n.* Ingredients, component parts; pillars, props.

আরজ, A. *n.* A petition, a request, a complaint.

আরজ দাখিল করা, A. *v.* To file a petition, to present a request.

আরজবাশ্ৎ, A. *n.* A written petition.

আরজবেগী, A. *n.* One who reads petitions at court.

আর্‌জান, P *adv.* Cheap.

আর্‌জানী, P. *n.* Cheapness: a good harvest.

আরজী, A. *n.* A petition, a plaint.

আরজী-নবীস, A. *n.* One who writes out petitions.

আর্‌জু, P. *n.* A wish, a desire: a prayer, a request.

আর্‌জুমন্দ, P. *adj.* Wishful, desirous fond.

আর্‌বাব, A. *n.* Lords, possessors.

আরব, A. *n.* Arabia.

আরবী, A. *adj.* Arabic. *n.* The Arabic language.

আরমান, P. *n.* Longing, wish: eagerness; repentance.

আরশ, P. *n.* A throne.

আরাম, P *n.* Recovery, rest, health.

আরাম হওয়া, P. *v.* To recover (health).

আরাম করা, P. *v.* To heal.

আরাস্তা, P. *adj.* Prepared, arranged; adorned.

আরাস্তা করা, P. *v.* To settle, to arrange, to organize.

আরী, P. *n.* A small saw.

আরেন্দা, P. *n.* One who carries rents or taxes to the treasury.

আল্, A. The Arabic definite article, as আল্-কোরাণ, The Quran.

আল্ওয়ান, H. *n.* A shawl, a cloth.

আল্কাতরা, A. *n.* Tar, pitch.

আলকাব, A. *n.* Titles; addresses of letters.

আল্খেল্লা, (T. আল্খালক) A coat, a loose frock reaching to the knees.

আল্‌গা, H. *adj.* Disconnected, detached, separated, loose.

আলগোছ, (A. আল্গোজা) *n.* A musical instrument, a pipe.

আল্‌তাম্মা, *n.* Perpetual rent-free land.

আল্‌বত্তা, A. *adv.* Certainly, necessarily. (Sometimes written আল্‌বৎ)

আলবেল্লা, P. *n.* A long-stemmed tobacco-pipe.

আলাৎ, A. *n.* Tools, apparatus; movable or immovable property.

আলম, A. *n.* The world, the earth; a banner.

আলমগীর, A. *adj.* Conqueror of the world.

আলশিরা, *n.* Summit.

আলা, A. *adj.* High, most high.

আল্লাহ, A. *n.* The Supreme God, *Allah.* (Often written আল্লা).

আলামৎ, A. *n.* A sign, a mark.

আলাই, A. *n.* Misfortune, calamity.

আলাই বালাই, A. *n.* Various misfortunes.

আলাহিদা, P. *adj.* Separate. *adv.* Separately.

আলী, A. *n.* Muhammad's son-in-law *adj.* High, sublime, great.

আলীশান, A. *adj.* Splendid, grand, magnificent.

আল্‌কা, A. *n.* Pension, stipend, subsistence money.

আলেম, A. *adj.* Learned, wise. *n.* A learned man.

আশক, A. *n.* A lover, a suitor.

আশ্‌কারা P. *adj* Clear, apparent, known, conspicuous.

আশ্‌কারা করা, P. *v.* To reveal, to make known, to explain.

আশ্‌না, P. *n.* A friend, a companion. *adj.* Familiar, intimate.

আশ্‌নাই, P. *n.* Familiarity, intimacy, friendship.

আশ্‌রাফ, A. *n.* Nobles, grandees, people of good birth.

আশ্‌রাফৎ, A. *n.* Good breeding, politeness.

আশ্‌হাদ, A. *n.* Witnesses.

আস্‌ওদ, A. *adj.* Black.

আসওয়ার, P. *n.* A horseman, a rider, a trooper.

আস্‌ওয়ার হওয়া, P. *n.* To ride.

আস্‌ওয়ারী, P. *n.* The act of riding, horsemanship ; a cavalcade.

আস্‌তীন, P. *n.* The sleeve of a garment.

আস্‌বাব, A. *n.* Utensils, goods, chattels, baggage.

আস্‌মান, P. *n.* Heaven, the sky.

আসমানী, P. *adj.* Heavenly ; azure.

আসর, A. *n.* Time, age ; the afternoon ; the Muslim prayer said in the late afternoon ; a mark, an impression ; a result ; the Traditions of Islam.

আসল, A. *adj.* Real, genuine. *n.* Origin, source ; essence ; a capital sum of money, the principal.

আসলতন, A. *adv.* Personally, in person.

আসলী, A. *adj* Original, primary.

আস্‌হাব, A. *n.* Companions, friends ; *esp.* used of the immediate companions or disciples of Muhammad.

আসা, A. *n.* A rod, a staff, a mace.

আসাবরদার, A. *n.* A mace-bearer.

আসান, P. *adj.* Easy, smooth,

আসান করা, P. *v.* To alleviate, to make easy ; to remove a difficulty.

আসানী, P. *n.* Ease, felicity, rest ; freedom.

আসামী, A. *n.* A culprit, a defendant; and inhabitant ; a tenant. শিকামী আসামী, A sub-tenant.

আসীর, A. *n.* A prisoner, a captive.

আসীলৎ, A. *n.* A man's whole property.

আহ্দা, P. *adj.* Filled, satisfied.

আস্তর, P. *n.* Plaster; lining.

আস্তানা, P. *n.* A place where a Muslim saint resides; a door, an entrance to a shrine.

আস্তানা করা, P. *v.* To reside.

আস্তাবল, A. *n.* A stable.

আস্তীন, P. *n.* A sleeve.

আস্তে, (P. আহিস্তা), *adv.* Slowly, softly.

আহ্ওয়াল, A. *n.* States, conditions.

আহ্কাম, A. *n.* Commands, precepts.

আহ্মক, A. *adj.* Foolish, stupid. (Often written আহম্মক).

আহ্মকী, A. *n.* Foolishness; a fool, a simpleton.

আহল, A. *n.* People, race: an individual. আহল উল্-কেতাব, The People of the Book, *ie.* Jews and Christians আহল-উল্-সুন্নৎ, Followers of the traditional law of Islam.

আহাদীস, A. *n.* Traditions. (*plu.* of হদীস).

আহ্সান, A. *adj.* Beautiful, excellent.

ই

ইক্তিদার, A. *n.* Power, authority, rank.

ইক্বাল, A. *n.* Admission, confession; acceptance (of a bond &c).

ইক্রার, A. *n.* A statement, a confession; a promise; a settlement, a ratification, a receipt.

ইক্রারী, A. *n.* One who consents or confesses *adj.* Promissory.

ইক্রার করা, A. *v.* To promise; to assert; to confess.

ইক্রারনামা, A. *n.* A written statement or contract; an agreement.

ইক্রাম, A. *n.* Honour, respect.

ইকামৎ, A. *n.* Sojourn, act of staying in a place.

ইখ্তিয়ার, A. *n.* Choice; power, authority, jurisdiction.

ইখ্তিয়ার করা, A. *v.* To choose, to determine; to undertake.

ইখ্তিয়ারী, A. *adj.* Subject to choice, arbitraty.

ইখ্তিয়ারনামা, A. *n.* Power of attorney.

ইখ্তিলাফ, A. *n.* Contravention, contradiction, opposition, disagreement.

ইখ্তিলাফ রাখা, A. *v.* To disagree, to differ.

ইখ্রাজ, A. *n.* Expulsion; a turning out of possession.

ইখ্লাস, A. *n.* Sincerity; purity; friendship.

ইজ্তিহাদ, A. *n.* Effort, exertion.

ইজ্ন্, , A. *n.* Permission.

ইজননামা, A. *n.* Written permission; a will, a testament.

ইজ্মা, A. *n.* Assembly; unanimity in religious doctrine.

ইজ্মাল, A. *n.* Sum, substance: joint possession; a summary, an abstract.

ইজ্মালী, A. *adj.* Joint, held in common; abridged.

ইজ্মালী মহল, A. *n.* An estate held in common by various heirs.

ইজ্‌লাস, A. *n.* A sitting in court, a session.

ইজ্‌লাসখানা A. *n.* A court room.

ইজ্‌হার, A. *n.* A declaration; an affidavit, deposition of a witness.

ইজ্‌হার দেওয়া, A. *v.* To depose, to declare.

ইজা, P. *n.* Carried forward (in accounts)

ইজাজৎ, A. *n.* Sanction, permission.

ইজাদ, P. *n.* Invention.

ইজাফা, A. *n.* Addition, increase.

ইজার, P. *n.* Trowsers, drawers.

ইজারবন্দ, P. *n.* That with which drawers are tied on.

ইজারা, A. *n.* A lease, a contract, a monopoly, a farm.

ইজারা দেওয়া, A. *v.* To farm or lease out.

ইজারাদার, A. *n.* A farmer; the holder of a contract or tenure; the holder of a monopoly.

ইজারাদারী, A. *n.* The occupation of an *Ijaradar*.

ইজারানামা, A. *n.* A lease; the document under which a lease is held.

ইজারা পাট্টা, A. *n.* A lease by which a whole village, several plots of land, or a whole market is let out for a specified time.

ইজালা, A. *n.* Removal, abolition.

ইজালা করা, A. *v.* To remove, to put away.

ইজাহার—*See* **ইজহার**

ইজ্জৎ, A. *n.* Honour, reputation.

ইঞ্জীল, A. *n.* The Gospel, the *Injil*. Sometimes used for the whole New Testament.

ইৎমাম, A. *n.* Completion, perfection.

ইৎলা—*See* **এৎলা**.

ইতায়েৎ, A. *n.* Submission.

ইত্তিবা, A. *n.* Obedience, submission.

ইত্তিফাক, A. *n.* Agreement, union.

ইত্তিলা, A. *n.* Information, notice, report, intelligence.
(Often written **এত্তিলা** and **এৎলা**)

ইত্তিলা করা, A. *v.* To notify, to announce, to give notice.

ইত্তিলানামা, A. *n.* A written report, a summons; a written declaration.

ইত্তিহাদ, A. *n.* Union, combination; treaty.

ইদ্দৎ, A. *n.* Period, time; *esp.* the time after the death of a Muhammadan during which his widow may not marry.

ইন্‌কার, A. *n.* Denial, refusal, contradiction, disagreement.

ইন্‌কার করা, A. *v.* To deny, to refuse.

ইন্‌কিসাম, A. *n.* Division, partition.

ইন্‌ফিসাল, A. *n.* Decision, sentence, award.

ইন্‌য়াম, A. *n.* A gift, benefaction; reward.

ইন্‌সান, A. *n.* A man.

ইন্‌সানীয়ৎ, A. *n.* Humanity.

ইন্‌সাফ, A. *n.* Equity, justice; decision.

ইন্‌সাফ করা, A. *v.* To decide, to administer justice.

ইনায়ৎ, A. *n.* Grace, favour; a gift.

ইন্তিকাম, A. *n.* Revenge, retaliation.

ইন্তিকাল, A. *n.* Death; removal transfer.

ইন্তিকাল করা, A. *v.* To die.

ইন্তিজাম, A. *n.* Arrangements, administration, order.

ইন্তিজাম করা, A. *v.* To arrange; to administer, to carry out.

ইন্তিজার, A. *n.* Expectation, hope.

ইন্তিহা A. *n.* Conclusion, termination, end.

ইন্তিহাম, A. *n.* Examination, test.

ইন্দারা, H. *n.* A large masonry well.

ইফ্‌তার, A. *n.* The breaking of the fast.

ইফ্‌রীৎ, P. *n.* A demon, an evil spirit.

ইফ্‌তিরা, A. *n.* Calumny, scandal.

ইব্‌তিদা, A. *n.* Beginning.

ইবন, A. *n.* A son.

ইব্‌রায়া, A. *n.* Remission, relinquishment, acquittance.

ইব্রাহীম, A. *n.* Abraham.

ইব্‌লীস, A. *n.* Satan, the devil.

ইম্‌তানায়া, A. Injunction, prohibition.

ইম্‌তিহান, A. *n.* Test, examination, experiment.

ইম্‌তিহানী, A. *adj.* Experimental.

ইম্‌দাদ, A. *n.* The act of helping; a gift.

ইম্‌লা, A. *n.* Orthography, dictation.

ইম্‌লাক, A. *n.* Property, possession.

ইমান, A. *n.* Faith, belief.

ইমান আনা, A. *n.* To believe, to exercise faith.

ইমানদার, A. *adj.* One having faith, believing.

ইমানদারী, A. *n.* The exercise of faith.

ইমাম, A. *n.* A priest; a leader of Muhammadan prayers; a title of the early Khalifs.

ইমামৎ, A. *n.* Priesthood; leadership.

ইমামবারা P. *n.* A building in which the *Mohurrum* is celebrated.

ইমারৎ, A. *n.* Authority, rule; dignity; magnificence. (See further under এমারৎ).

ইয়াজ্‌জ, A. *n.* Gog. (See further under মাজ্‌জ.)

ইয়াদ, A. *n.* Remembrance, recollection.

ইয়াদ রাখা, A. *n.* To bear in mind, to remember.

ইয়াদদস্ত, P. *n.* Memorandum.

ইয়ার, P. *n.* A friend, a companion.

ইয়ারী, P. *n.* Friendship.

ইয়ুনস, A. *n.* Jonah.

ইয়ুনানী. A. *n.* Greek. The Greek language.

ইয়েতীম, A. *n.* An orphan. (Often written এতিম).

ইর্‌শাদ, A. *n.* Direction, instruction; command; will.

ইর্‌শাদ করা, A. *v.* To guide, to direct; to order.

ইর্‌সাল, A. *n.* The sending of anything; a mission, a deputation; a remittance; despatch.

ইরাদা A. *n.* A wish, a desire; intention, resolve; object in view. (Also written এরাদা)

ইল্‌তেজা, A. *n.* Importunity, supplication, entreaty.

ইল্‌তেজা করা, A. *v.* To entreat, to request.

ইল্‌বাস, A. *n.* Clothes, garments.

ইলম্‌, A. *n.* Science; knowledge, wisdom.

ইলমবাজ, A. *adj.* Wise, clever,

ইলমদার, A. *adj.* Wise, clever.

ইল্‌হাম, A. *n.* Inspiration, revelation.

ইলাকা—*See* এলাকা.

ইলাহ্‌, A. *n.* A god, a divinity.

ইলাহী, A. *adj.* Divine.

ইলাহীয়ৎ, A. *n.* Divinity.

ইল্লৎ, A. *n.* Cause; vice; rubbish, filth.

ইল্লৎখানা, A. *n.* A privy.

ইল্লতী, A. *adj.* Filthy, abominable.

ইশ্‌তিরাক, A. *n.* Partnership.

ইশ্‌তেহার, A. *n.* Proclamation, notice, announcement; a handbill. (Often written এস্তাহার).

ইশ্‌তেহার দেওয়া, A. *v.* To announce, to give notice, to publish.

ইশ্‌তেহারনামা, A. *n.* A written proclamation.

ইশ্‌রাক A. *n.* The rising of the sun.

ইশা—*See* এশা.

ইশাদী, P. *n.* A witness.

ইশারা, A. *n.* A sign; a clue, allusion, hint.

ইশারা করা, A. *v.* To beckon, to sign, to point out; to hint, to refer to.

ইসম্‌ A. *n.* A name.

ইসম্‌-নবীস, A. *n.* One who writes down a list of names.

ইস্‌মায়েল, A. *n.* Ishmael.

ইস্‌রাফীল, A. *n.* The angel of death.

ইস্‌লাম, A. *n.* *Islam.* The religion founded by Muhammad.

ইস্‌লামী, A. *adj.* Pertaining to Islam.

ইস্‌লাহ্‌, A. *n.* Correction, revision, improvement.

ইস্‌হাক, A. *n.* Isaac.

ইসা, A. *n.* *Isa.* Jesus.

ইসাই, A. *n.* A Christian.

ইস্তক, H. *adv.* To this (place), hither; from. (Properly ইস্‌ তক).

ইস্তক নাগাইদ, H. *adv.* Inclusive, from this to that.

ইস্তাহার—*See* ইশ্‌তেহার

ইস্তিগ্‌ফার, A. *n.* Asking forgiveness.

ইস্তিগ্‌ফার আল্লাহ A. *Int.* I ask forgiveness of God!

ইস্তিদ্‌রাক A. *n.* Acquisition; overtaking; improving.

ইস্তিন্‌জা, A. *n.* Purification.

ইস্তিফা, A. *n.* Asking forgiveness; resignation, relinquishment.

ইস্তিক্‌সার, A. *n.* A question, enquiry investigation, reference.

ইস্তিম্‌রার, A. *n.* Permanence; a fixed rent.

ইস্তিম্‌রারী, A. *adj.* Perpetual, permanent. *n.* Land held at a fixed rent.

ইস্তিম্‌রারদার, A. *n.* The holder of a permanent lease at a fixed rent.

ইস্তিমাল, A. *n.* Custom, practice, habit, use.

ইস্তিমাল করা, A. *v.* To use, to exercise, to employ.

ইস্তিহ্‌কাক, A. *n.* Claim, right, title.

ইস্তিহ্‌লাফ, A. *n.* Causing to swear.

ইস্রায়েল A. *n.* Israel.

ইহ্‌তিয়াজ, A. *n.* Need, anxiety, urgency.

ইহ্তিমাম, A. *n.* Responsibility, care, control, supervision, superintendence.

ইহ্তিমাম করা, A. *v.* To superintend, to administer, to manage.

ইহ্তিমামদার, P. *n.* One having responsibility.

ইহ্তিরাজ, A. *n.* Abstinence.

ইহ্রাম, A. *n.* A special garment worn by pilgrims on entering Mecca to perform the *haj.*

ইহ্সান, A. *n.* Benevolence; kindness favour.

ইহ্সানমন্দ, A. *adj.* Grateful, thankful

ইহ্সানমন্দী, A. *n.* Gratitude.

ইহাতা, A. *n.* Enclosure, compound.

ঈ

ঈজার, A. *n.* Affirmation, consent.

ঈদ, A. *n.* A festival, a feast.

ঈদ-উল্-ফিতর, The feast of breaking the fast at *Ramadhan.*

ঈদ-উল্-জুহা, The feast of sacrifice. In Bengal the latter is commonly called the *Bakr Id.*

ঈদগাহ, A. *n.* The building in which the *Id* is performed; a place where *Id* prayers are said.

ঈদী, A. *n.* A present made at the time of the *Id.*

উ

উকালৎ—*See* ওকালৎ

উকীল, A. *n.* *Vakeel*, a pleader; an envoy, an agent.

উকীলী, A. *n.* Pleadership; agency.

উকুবৎ, A. *n.* Punishment.

উজ্বক, T. *n.* A Tartar; a fool, a simpleton.

উজাড়, H. *n.* Waste, destruction; *adj.* Wasted, destroyed, demolished; uninhabited.

উজালা, H. *n.* Daylight, sunlight, dawn; splendour, brightness. *adj.* Bright, shining.

উজীর, A. *n.* A *vizier*, a minister of state.

উজীরী, A. *n.* The office of a *vizier.*

উজু—*See* ওজু.

উঠবন্দী পাট্টা, H. *n.* A lease covering one season's crops only.

উঠবন্দী রাইয়ৎ, H. *n.* A tenant who rents land for one year only.

উতরিয়া যাওয়া, H. *v.* To descend.

উদ্বাস্ত জমী, H. *n.* Land which is contiguous to homestead land.

উদ্বাস্ত করা, H. *v.* To eject from homestead land.

উম্মাদ, A. A representative.

উম্, A. *n.* A mother.

উমর, A. *n.* Age; time.

উমর ভোর A. *adv.* For life, lifelong.

উমরা, A. *n.* Noblemen, grandees. (*Plu.* of আমীর).

উম্মৎ, A. *n.* Disciple; people of the same faith; religious sect.

উম্মতী, A. *n.* A believer in or follower of any religious sect.

উম্মী, A. *adj.* Ignorant, *esp.* unacquainted with the Jewish and C istian scriptures.

উম্মেদ, P. *n.* Expectation, hope.

উম্মেদওয়ার, P. *adj.* Hopeful, expectant.

উম্মেদওয়ারী, P. *n.* Hopefulness, expectancy.

উম্মেদদার, P. *adj.* Hopeful, expectant : a candidate for employment.

উম্মেদবারী, P. *n* Hopefulness, expectancy.

উর্দ্দু, P. *n.* The name given to the language used by Muslims in N. W. India. *adj.* Belonging to the camp.

উল্‌ফৎ, A. *n.* Friendship, affection.

উল্‌ফৎ করা, A. *v.* To make friendship with any one ; to be intimate with any one.

উলমা, A. *n.* Learned men. (Often written ওলামা).

উস্তাদ—*See* ওস্তাদ

উসুল, A. *n.* Principles, laws ; doctrines ; sources, origins ; collection or realization of revenue.

উসুল করা, A. *v.* To collect or realize revenue.

উসুলবাকী, A. *n.* Collection of arrears or balances.

উস্‌বাস, A. *n.* Doubt, hesitation ; whispering suggestions of the devil.

উস্‌বাস করা, A. *v.* To hesitate, to waver.

এ

এওজ, A. *n.* Change, exchange ; substitute.

এওজে, A. *adv.* In exchange, instead of.

একজাই, P. *n.* A bringing together : a total.

একজাই করা, P. *v.* To collect, to bring together.

একজাই চালান, P. *n.* A statement of remittances made to a zemindar.

একতরফ, P. *adv.* On the same side.

একতরফা, P. *adj.* One-sided, partial, *ex parte.*

একদম, P. *n.* One breath. *adv.* Altogether ; at once, outright.

একরার—*See* ইকরার.

একলৌটা, H. *adj.* Only begotten.

একামৎ—*See* ইকামৎ.

একেলা, H. *adj.* Single, alone (Also written একলা and একালা)

একিদা—*See* আকীদা

একীন, A. *n.* Belief ; confidence, assurance. *adj.* Sure, certain.

একীন করা, A. *v.* To believe ; to rely on.

একুন, H. *n.* Sum, total. *adv.* In all, altogether.

একোয়াল খতিয়ান, *n.* A zemindary document showing a summary of the details regarding lands let to tenants.

এগানগী, H. *n.* Singleness, peerlessness.

এগানা, H. *adj.* Sole, single, unique.

এজ্‌মাল—*See* ইজ্‌মাল

এজ্‌রা, A. *n.* Performance, execution.

এজ্‌লাস—*See* ইজ্‌লাস.

এজ্‌হার—*See* ইজ্‌হার.

এজাজৎ—*See* ইজাজৎ.

এৎনা, H. *adv.* So much.

এতমাম, *n.* The farming out of lands or dues.

এতমামদার, *n.* One who farms out land to under-tenants.

এতমামদারী, *n.* The profession of farming out land to under-tenants.

এৎমীনান্, A. *n.* Rest, tranquility, peace.

এতিকাদ, A. *n.* Belief, trust, reliance.

এতিকাফ, A. *n.* Retirement to a mosque or other place for purposes of religious contemplation.

এতিম—*See* ইয়েতীম

এতিমাদ, A. *n.* Reliance, dependence upon.

এতিরাজ, A. *n.* Objection, criticism, dispute.

এস্তেলা—*See* ইস্তেলা

এনায়েৎ, A. *n.* Favour, support.

এস্তেকাল—*See* ইস্তিকাল

এফ্তার—*See* ইফ্তার

এবরা *n.* Exclusion, rejection. *adj.* Rejected.

এবাদৎ, A. *n.* Worship; service.

এবাদৎ করা, A. *v.* To worship, to serve.

এবাদৎখানা, A. *n.* A temple, a place of worship.

এবাদৎগাহ, A. *n.* A temple, a place of worship.

এবারৎ, A. *n.* The text of a book; idiom, style; a reading.

এমাম—*See* ইমাম

এমারৎ A. *n.* An edifice, a masonry building.

এরাদা—*See* ইরাদা

এল্বাস—*See* ইলবাস

এলাইচ, P. *n.* A cardamom.

এলাকা, A. *n.* Connection, relation; jurisdiction; a holding, a district; tenure.

এলাকাদার, A. *adj.* Having connection with another.

এলাজ, A. *n.* Cure, relief.

এলাজ করা, A. *v.* To cure.

এলেম—*See* ইল্‌ম্.

এশা, A. *n.* The first watch of the night; the fifth of the Muslim canonical prayers, said after nightfall.

এস্রাজ, P. *n.* A stringed musical instrument.

এস্তাওয়া, *n.* Progressive rate of rent on new land.

এস্তাহার—*See* ইশ্‌তেহার

ও

ওইরাসৎ, A. *n.* Inheritance, hereditary right.

ওইলায়ৎ, A. *n.* *Vilayat*, a district, a province; *Bilat*, a foreign country (?).

ওকফ, A. *n.* A Muhammadan religious or charitable endowment.

ওকফনামা, A. *n.* A written deed of endowment.

ওকর, A. *n.* Dignity honour.

ওকালৎ, A. *n.* The profession of a *vakeel* or attorney; agency. (Often written ওকালতী).

ওকালৎনামা, A. *n.* Written power of attorney; the document conferring a power of attorney.

ওকালতী করা, A. *n.* To practise the profession of a *vakeel*,

ওকূ, A. *n.* An occurrence, an event.

ওকূ হওয়া, A. *v.* To happen.

ওকূফ, A. *n.* Sense, understanding; intellect.

ওকূয়াৎ, A. *n.* Events, occurrences.

ওক্ত, (A. ওক্‌ৎ) *n.* Time, term, season.

ওক্তিয়া, A. *adj.* Timely, seasonable.

ওগাইরহ্‌ A. *Et cetera*, and the like.

ওজন, A. *n.* Measure, weight.

ওজন করা, A. *v.* To weigh.

ওজনদার, A. *n.* A measurer, a weighman.

ওজর. A. *n.* Excuse. apology; reason, objection.

ওজর করা, A. *v.* To make an objection, to apologise.

ওজরদার, A. *n.* Objector, claimant.

ওজরদারী A. *n.* Claim.

ওজহ্‌, A. *n.* Reason, cause; excuse; face; means.

ওজহ্‌নামা, A. *n.* A written statement of the causes of complaint.

ওজারৎ, A. *n.* The office of a *vizier*; the ministry.

ওজীফৎ, A. *n.* Muhammadan daily worship; stipend, pension; gift of land for services rendered.

ওজীর, A. *n.* A *vizier*, a minister of state.

ওজূ, A. *n.* Ablution (before prayer).

ওজূহাৎ, A. *n.* Reasons, excuses; objections, (*Plu.* of ওজহ্‌)

ওজূদ, A. *n.* Being, existence, life; substance.

ওতন, A. *n.* Birthplace, one's native country; a dwelling.

2

ওদুল, A. *n.* Disobedience, insubordination, violation.

ওদুল করা, A. *v.* To violate (a law or rule;) to disobey; to break (a promise).

ওদূদ, A. *n.* A lover.

ওফা, A. *n.* Keeping a promise, fidelity.

ওফাৎ, A. *n.* Death.

ওফাৎ করা, A. *v.* To die.

ওম্‌দা, A. *n.* A grandee. *adj.* Good, rich.

ওমর—*See* উমর.

ওম্‌রা, A. *n.* The lesser pilgrimage to Mecca.

ওয়াকফ—*See* ওক্‌ফ.

ওয়াকিফ, A. *adj.* Aware of, acquainted with.

ওয়াকিফহাল, A. *n.* An experienced person.

ওয়াকূয়া—*See* ওকূ.

ওয়াকূফ—*See* ওকূফ.

ওয়াজ, A. *n.* Preaching; (Commonly used in the sense of discussion)

ওয়াজ করা, A. *n.* To preach.

ওয়াজিব, A. *adj.* Right, proper; obligatory; necessary; due.

ওয়াজিবী, A. *n.* Expediency; fitness.

ওয়াদা, A. *n.* A promise an agreement.

ওয়াদা করা, A. *v.* To promise, to agree to.

ওয়াদী, A. *n.* A valley, a *wady*.

ওয়াপস, P. *adv.* Back, again. *n.* a returning.

ওয়াপস করা, P. *v.* To refund, to pay back.

ওয়াপস দেওয়া—Same as ওয়াপস করা.

ওয়াপসী, P. *n.* A return, a refund.
ওয়ায়েজ, A. *n.* A preacher.
ওয়ারিস, A. *n.* An heir, an owner.
ওয়ারিস করা, A. *v.* To inherit.
ওয়ারিসান, A. *n.* Heirs.
ওয়ালা, H. *n.* A suffix denoting the doer, agent, possessor etc., as পানী-ওয়ালা, a man who carries water.
ওয়ালী—*See* অলী.
ওয়ালেদ, A. *n.* Father.
ওয়ালেদা, A. *n.* Mother.
ওয়াসিল, A. *n.* Realization, collection; receipts. *adj.* Arrived at; joined to; received.
ওয়াসিল বাকী, A. *n.* A statement of rent receipts and of rents due; balances.
ওয়াসিল বাকী করা, A. *v.* To balance an account.
ওয়াসিলাৎ, A. *n.* The proceeds of an estate.
ওয়াস্তা, A. *n.* A medium, an instrument; account, sake; a reason.
ওয়াস্তে, A. *adv.* For the sake of, on behalf of.
ওয়াহেদ, A. *adj.* One.
আল্-ওয়াহেদ, A. *n.* God.
ওয়াহেব, A. *n.* A giver, a donor.
ওরক, A. *n.* A leaf, a page, a sheet of paper.
ওরৎ—*See* ঔরৎ.
ওর্ফে, A. Otherwise called, *alias.*
ওরাসৎ, A. *n.* Heirship, inheritance.
ওলদ, A. *n.* A boy, a son.
ওলদীয়ৎ, A. *n.* Pedigree, descent.
ওলাদৎ, A. *n.* Birth.
ওস্ওয়াস্, A. *n.* Doubt, suspicion; temptations of the devil.
ওস্ওয়াসী, A. *adj.* Suspicious.
ওসৎ, A. *adj.* Middle. A term applied to a tenure of land held from a superior landlord.
ওসৎ তালুক, A. *n.* A portion of a *taluk* held in subordination to an entire *taluk.*
ওসৎ হাওয়ালা, A. *n.* A tenure subordinate to a *hawata* lease.
ওসী, A. *n.* An executor.
ওসীয়ৎ, A. *n.* A will, a testament; a command.
ওসীয়ৎ নামা, A. *n.* A written will.
ওসীয়ৎ করা, A. *v.* To bequeath.
ওসীলা, A. *n.* Means; pretext; intervention; patronage.
ওসীলাদার, A. *n.* A dependant, a client.
ওসীলায়, A. *adv.* By means of.
ওস্তওয়ার, P. *adj.* Strong, firm, level.
ওস্তাগর, P. *n.* A tailor; a teacher; a skilled artizan.
ওস্তাগরী, P. *n.* The craft of a tailor.
ওস্তাদ, P. *n.* A teacher, a preceptor, a master; one skilled in anything.
ওস্তাদী, P. *n.* Teachership, mastership.
ওস্তাদী করা, P. *v.* To pretend to expert knowledge; to interfere.
ওহদ—*See* অহদ.
ওহাবী, A. *n.* A sect of Muslims. The *Wahabis.*
ওহী, A. *n.* Inspiration, revelation.
ঔরৎ, A. A woman, a wife.

ক

কওয়াল, A. *n.* A musician.

কওয়ালী, A. *n.* A musical measure.

কইসর, A. *n.* An emperor ; Caesar.

কইসর-ই-হিন্দ *n.* A decoration conferred by the India Government.

কওয়ায়েদ, A. *n.* Rules and regulations ; laws ; principles ; drill.

কএদ—*See* কয়েদ.

কজব—*See* কিজব.

কজীয়া, A. *n.* A dispute, a quarrel, a law-case ; a proposition.

কড়চা, H. *n.* Statement of rent paid or outstanding.

কট, H. *adj.* Conditional. *n.* a stipulation.

কটকিনা, H. *n.* A sub-lease ; land which is sublet—generally for one year.

কটকিনা দেওয়া, H. *v.* To sublet.

কটকিনাদার, H. *n.* One who leases land for a limited period of time.

কটকবালা, A. *n.* A conditional mortgage or sale.

কৎ, A. *n.* The nib of a pen.

কতরা, A. *n.* A drop.

কতল, A. *n.* Murder, slaughter.

কতল করা, A. *v.* To kill, to execute.

কতা, A. *n.* A piece, a share ; a section ; a plot.

কতার, A. *n.* A row, a file ; a procession.

কদম, A. *n.* A foot ; a step.

কদর, A. *n.* Fate, destiny ; a quantity, a portion ; merit, appreciation ; honour, greatness.

কদর করা, A. *v.* To appreciate, to esteem.

কদামৎ, A. *n.* Age, antiquity.

কদীম, A. *adj.* Old, ancient.

কদ্দ স—*See* কুদ্দ স.

কন্দকার, P. *n.* An engraver.

কফন, A. *n.* A shroud, a coffin.

কফনী, A. *n.* A dress of Muslim beggars.

কফারা, A. *n.* Expiation, atonement. (Often written কাফারা).

কফারা করা, A. *v.* To make atonement, to make expiation.

কফালৎ, A. *n.* Bail, security.

কফীলা, A. *n.* A caravan.

কব, H. *adv.* When ?

কবচ—*See* কবজ.

কবজ, A. *n.* A grasp ; taking possession, sequestration ; a receipt.

কবজ করা, A. *v.* To take possession of ; to conquer.

কব্জা, A. *n.* A hinge ; the wrist ; a grip of the hand.

কব্জা দেওয়া, A. *v.* To make over charge ; to give delivery.

কব্জা রাখা, A. *v.* To keep, to retain.

কব্জাদারী, A. *n.* Occupancy.

কবর, A. *n.* A grave.

কবরস্থান, A. *n.* A graveyard, a cemetary.

কবর দেওয়া, A. *v.* To bury.

কবা, A. *n.* A long gown.

কবাপোশ, A. *n.* A long gown.

কবাব, P. *n.* Roasted meat.

কবালা, A. *n.* A bill of sale ; a deed of transfer ; a bond : title deeds.

কটকবালা, A conditional deed of sale.

খুশকবালা, An unconditional agreement or sale.

কবীর, A. *adj.* Great, distinguished.

কবীরা, A. *n.* Great sins, mortal sins. (Muslim divines differ as to their number and names.)

কবীল, A. *n.* Surety, bail.

কবীলা, A. *n.* Tribe, clan; wife; family.

কবূতর, P. *n.* A pigeon.

কবূতর-খানা, P. *n.* A pigeon-house.

কবূল, A. *n.* An acknowledgment, an acceptance; consent, an agreement, a promise.

কবূল করা, A. *n.* To acknowledge, to consent to; to accept, to receive.

কবূলতী—See কবূলীয়ৎ.

কবূলাবেশী, A. *n.* An agreement to pay more rent than that stipulated in the *kabuliyat*.

কবূলীয়ৎ, A. *n.* A counter-lease, a deed of agreement given by a tenant to the landlord; a deed of acceptance. (Often written কবূলতী.)

কভী, H. *adv.* At any time.

কম, P. *adj.* Little, few; less; deficient. (Used much in compounds as কম্‌-জোর, of little strength, weak.

কমক, P. *n.* Aid, reinforcement; an assistant, an associate.

কম্‌জোর, P. *adj.* Weak, feeble.

কম্‌জোরী, P. *n.* Weakness. [fect.

কম্‌তী, P. *n.* Littleness, paucity, de-

কমবখৎ, P. *adj.* Unlucky; unfortunate.

কম্‌বেশ, P. *adv.* More or less, thereabouts.

কমর, P. *n.* The loins, the waist. (Often written কোমর). A. The moon.

কমরী, A. *adj.* Lunar.

কমরকুশাই, P. *n.* A fee paid to a peon.

কমরবন্দ, P. *n.* A girdle for the loins, a belt.

কমা, P. *v.* To lessen, to be reduced.

কমান, P. *n.* A bow; an arch. *v.* To lessen, to diminish.

কমাল, A. *adj.* Perfect. *n.* Perfection.

কমী, P. *n.* Littleness, defectiveness, deficiency, reduction.

কমীনা, P. *adj.* Vulgar, common, base, vile. *n.* The common people.

কমীনাপান, P. *n.* A base person.

কম্বল, A. *n.* A blanket.

কয়য়াল, A. *n.* One who measures or weighs.

কয়য়ালদার, A. *n.* One who measures or weighs.

কয়য়ালী A. *n.* The work or business of a *kayyal*, or his fee.

কয়েদ, A. *n.* Imprisonment, confinement.

কয়েদ করা, A. *v.* To imprison

কয়েদখানা, A. *n.* A jail.

কয়েদী, A. *n.* A prisoner in a jail.

করণেওয়ালা, H. *n.* The doer of an action.

করবলা, A. *n.* The place where the *taziya* in the Muhurram procession is buried; a burial ground.

করম, A. *n.* Graciousness, bounty, generosity.

করাবৎ, A. *n.* Near relationship.

করামৎ, A. *n.* Honour, dignity; a miracle performed by a saint (Often written কেরামৎ).

করামতী, A. *adj.* Miraculous.

করার, A. *n.* Firmness, consistency; patience; a promise, a contract; an engagement.

করার করা, A. *v.* To make an agreement, to promise; to take a stand, to determine.

করারী. A. *adj.* Fixed established; ratified, promised.

করারী পাট্টা, A conditional lease.

করারী জমী, Land the rent of which is paid in kind by a stipulated proportion of the crop.

করারনামা, A. *n.* A treaty.

করীব, A. *adj.* Near, adjacent.

করীম, A. *adj.* Bountiful, gracious; liberal.

কর্জ্জ, A. *n.* A loan, a debt.

কর্জ্জ করা, A. *v.* To borrow.

কর্জ্জ দেওয়া, A. *v.* To lend.

কর্জ্জদার, A. *n.* A debtor, a borrower.

কর্জ্জপত্র, A. *n.* A promissory note, bond.

কর্জ্জী, A. *n.* A debtor, a borrower.

কলগী T. *n.* A crest, a plume, a spire, a *tiara*.

কলন্দর, A. *n.* A monk, an ascetic.

কলব, A. *n.* The heart.

কলম, A. *n.* A pen.

কলমজারী, A. *adj.* Busy, engaged in work.

কলমতরাশ, A. *n.* A pen-knife.

কলমদান, A. *n.* A pen-case or stand.

কলমপেশা, A. *n.* Penmanship.

কলমবন্দ, A. *adj.* Written, inserted.

কলমবন্দ করা, A. *v.* To commit to writing, to make an entry.

কলমবাজ, A. *adj.* Skilled in writing.

কলমবাজী, A. *n.* Skill in writing.

কলিমা, A. *n.* A word; the Muhammadan confession of faith; 'There is no God but Allah, and Muhammad is the Apostle of Allah. (Often written **কলমা**).

কলিমা পড়া, A. *v.* To repeat the Muhammadan confession of faith. To embrace Islam.

কলিমা পড়ান, A. *v.* To publicly receive one into Islam.

কলীম, A. *n.* A speaker.

কলীম-উল্লাহ, the speaker with God; a title of Moses.

কলাই, A. *n.* The tinning or plating of cooking and other utensils. *adj.* Tinned, plated.

কলাই করা, A. *v.* To tin, to plate.

কলাইগর, A. *n.* A tin-plater.

কলাইগরী, A. *n.* The work of a tin-plater.

কলাম, A. *n.* A word.

কলী, A. *n.* Wet lime.

কলেজা, H. The heart; the liver; [courage.

কল্লা, P. *n.* A noise, a row.

কল্লাদরাজ, P. *adj.* Noisy; abusive.

কশফ, A. *n.* Revelation, manifestation.

কশফী, A. *adj.* Revealed, manifest.

কশমকশ, P. *n.* Distraction; jostling.

কশা, P. *v.* To work a sum, to solve a problem; to draw tight.

কশীদা, P. *adj.* Tight, pulled close. *n.* Embroidery.

কসদ, A. *n.* An attempt; intention.

কসদ করা, A. *v.* To attempt, to strive; to intend.

কসদান, A. *adv.* Wilfully.

কসব, A. *n.* Occupation, profession; skill.

কস্‌বা, A. *n.* A small town, a large village.

কস্‌বী, A. *n.* A prostitute.

কসবী খানা, A. *n.* A brothel.

কস্‌বীবাজ A. *n.* A rake, a profligate.

কসম, A. *n.* An oath.

কসম খাওয়া, A. *v.* To take an oath.

কসম দেওয়া, A. *v.* To adjure.

কসর, A. *n.* Damage, loss, defect.

কসরৎ, A. *n.* Exercise, drill, labour, practice, habit; a heap, a multitude (Sometimes written কসলৎ).

কসরতী, A. *adj.* Athletic.

কসাই, A. *n.* A butcher.

কসীদা, A. *n.* A kind of poetical composition.

কসুর, A. *n.* Fault; deficiency; defect.

কহর, A. *n.* Severity; indignation, anger; calamity, danger.

কাঁচি, T. *n.* A pair of scissors.

কাইজা—*See* কায়েজা.

কাউল—*See* কৌল.

কাওয়াজ, A. *n.* Drill, parade; discharge of firearms.

কাওয়াল—*See* কওয়াল.

কাগজ, A. *n.* Paper; a document.

কাগজী, A. *n.* A paper-maker; a stationer; records.

কাগজী-লেবু, A. A kind of lemon.

কাগজ-পত্র, A. *n.* Deeds, documents. খবরের কাগজ. A newspaper.

কাজা, (A. কজা) *n.* Death; fate; omission of a prayer or fast. (Often written কায়েজা.)

কাজা করা, A. *v.* To die; to omit to perform some obligatory religious duty.

কাজী, A. *n.* A Muhammadan judge.

কাজেব, A. *n.* A liar, *adj.* False.

কাতল, A. *n.* A killing; a murderer.

কাতার, (A. কতার) *n.* A line, a row, a procession.

কাতারে কাতারে, A. *adv.* In rows.

কাদের, A. *adj.* Powerful; able: competent.

কানাৎ, A. *n.* The walls of a tent; the back of a house, the space under the eaves of a house. (Also written কানাচ).

কানুন, A. *n.* Regulation, law, statute. আইন কানুন, laws and regulations.

কানুনগো A. *n.* A subordinate revenue officer; an officer in charge of public records.

কাফারা—*See* কফারা.

কাফী, A. *adj.* Sufficient, enough.

কাফিলা. A. *n.* A caravan.

কাফের, A. *n.* An infidel, a *kafir*.

কাফেরী, A. *n.* Infidelity.

কাফেল, A. *n.* One who gives bail; a surety.

কাবা, A. *n.* The *kaaba* or temple at Mecca.

কাবার, A. *n.* The end.

কাবাল—*See* কাওয়াল.

কাবীন, P. *n.* A marriage portion, a dower.

কাবীননামা, P. *n.* A deed of dower, a marriage settlement.

কাবেজ, A. *n.* A possessor, occupier.

কাবেজ করা, A. *v.* To control, to possess. (*See* under কবজ.)

কাবেল, A. *adj.* Able, capable; worthy, fit.

কাবু. T. *n.* Power, control, command; grip, hold. *adj.* Weak, prostrate, thin.

কাবু করা, T. *v.* To bring under control, to weaken.

কাবুলী, P. *n.* A resident of Cabul; made or grown in Cabul.

কাম, H. *n.* Work.

কামাই, P. *n.* Rest, absence, leisure; earnings.

কামাই করা, P. *v.* To absent oneself from duty.

কামান, (P. কমান) *n.* A bow; a gun, a cannon; earnings. *v.* To earn.

কামিজ, (A. কমীস). *n.* A shirt, a *chemise.*

কামেল, A. *adj.* Full, complete, perfect, absolute, entire.

কায়সা, H. *adv.* How; of what kind, why?

কায়েজা—*See* কাজা.

কায়েদা, A. *n.* Law, rule, habit, the established order of things; manner; means.

কায়েম, A. *adj.* Perpendicular; firm; permanent.

কায়েম মোকাম, A. *n.* Delegate, representative, deputy.

কায়েম করা, A. *v.* To make firm or permanent; to place upright.

কায়েম রাখা, A. *v.* To observe (a law).

কায়েমী, A. *adj.* Permanent, firm. *n.* Firmness, durableness; permanence. কায়েমী পাট্টা, a lease giving a permanent right.

কার, P. *n.* Work, act, function;

কারকিৎ, A. *n.* Cultivation.

কারকিৎ করা, *v.* To cultivate, to make land fit for cultivation.

কারকুন, P. *n.* An agent, a superintendent, a zemindari clerk who keeps accounts.

কারখানা, P. *n.* A factory, a workshop; an affair.

কারগুজার, P. *adj.* Expert; dutiful; expeditious.

কারগুজারী, P. *n.* Expertness.

কারপরদাজ, P. *n.* An agent; an officer.

কারবান, (P. কারওয়ান) *n.* A caravan.

কারবার, P. *n.* Business, trade; a transaction.

কারবারী, P. *adj.* Commercial. *n.* A man of business.

কারসাজ, P. *adj.* Deceitful, tricky.

কারসাজী, P. *n.* A fraud, a trick, cheating.

কারী, A. *n.* A reader. *esp.* a reader of the Quran.

কারিন্দা, P. *n.* A workman, an agent.

কারীগর, P. *n.* A workman a mechanic; a weaver.

কারীগরী, P. *n.* Workmanship, skill; mechanics; weaving.

কালবুদ, P. *n.* Form; the human body. (Sometimes written কালেব)

কালেব, A. *n.* A frame, the centre of an arch: a cobbler's last; the human body.

কাল্লা, P. *n.* Summit, top; head.

কাশৎ, P. *n.* Cultivated land; a tenure of land; cultivation.

কাশৎকার, P. *n.* A cultivator, a farmer.

কাসিদ, A. *n.* A messenger.

কাহেন, A. *n.* A sooth-sayer, a magician.

কাহেল, A. *adj.* Idle; weak, thin, [emaciated.

কিজব, A. *n.* A lie, a falsehood. (Also written কজর).

কিতা, A. *n.* A bit, a fragment, a share; a plot of land.

কিতা কিতা, A. *adv.* By pieces, by [lots.

কিতাহুরস্ত, A. *adj.* Well arranged.

কিতাদুরস্তী, A. *n.* Good arrangement.

কিতাব, A. *n.* A book. (Often written কেতাব).

কিতাবৎ, A. *n.* The act of writing; an inscription.

কিতাবখানা, A. *n.* A bookshop, a [library.

কিতাবী, A. *adj.* Pertaining to or possessing a Book: Jews and Christians.

কিতায় কিতায়, A. *adv.* Piece by piece.

কিনারা, P. *n.* Edge, border, shore, boundary.

কিনারা করা, P. *v.* To retire, to keep [aloof.

কিনারা রাখা, P. *v.* To put aside.

কিফায়ৎ, A. *n.* Gain, profit.

কিফায়তী, A. *adj.* Profitable. *n.* One who gains by trade.

কিব্‌লা, A *n.* The *kibla*; the direction in which Muslims pray; the temple at Mecca. Any great person as king, patron, sire. Your Majesty; কিব্‌লা দোজাহান, patron of both worlds.

কিমার, P. *n.* Dice, any game of hazard.

কিমারবাজ, P. *n.* A gambler.

কিমারবাজী, P. *n.* Gambling.

কিমিয়া, A. *n.* Chemistry.

কিয়া, H *pro.* What? *Int.* What!

কিম্‌খাব, (P. কমখুয়াব). *n.* Brocade.

কিয়াম, A. *n.* The standing position in Muslim liturgical prayer.

কিয়ামৎ, A. *n.* Resurrection, the last day.

কিয়াস, A. *n.* Thought, judgment, opinion, reasoning; a logica deduction.

কিয়াসী, A. *adj.* Imaginary, hypothetical.

কিরমিজ, A. *adj.* Scarlet, crimson.

কিরাৎ, A. *n.* Elocution; a recital of the Quran, a reading; a text.

কিরামৎ—*See* কিরামৎ.

কিরায়া—*See* কেরায়া.

কিশতী, P. *n.* A boat, a ship.

কিশতীবান, P. *n.* A boatman.

কিশ্‌মিশ, P. *n.* A raisin, a dried grape.

কিস্? H. *pro.* Who?, which?, what?

কিস্ত, A. *n.* Instalment, portion; the period for payment of an instalment: a dividend. (Sometimes written কিস্তি).

কিস্তবন্দী, A. *n.* Payment of revenue by instalments; the record of payments by instalments.

কিস্তখেলাফ, A. *n.* Failure to pay agreed instalments.

কিস্তখেলাফী, A. *adj.* Pertaining to unpaid dues.

কিস্‌ম্‌, A. *n.* A kind, sort, species; portion: nature, description.

কিস্‌মৎ, A. *n.* Fate, destiny; division of a village or district; share.

কিস্‌মৎনামা, A. *n.* A deed of partition.

কিস্‌মতী, *n.* Location. *adj.* Situated [in.

কিসস, A. *n.* Stories.

কিস্‌সা, A. *n.* A story, a history. (Sometimes written কেচ্ছা).

কিস্‌সাগো, A. *n.* A story-teller.

কিসাস, A. *n.* Retaliation, revenge: capital punishment.

কীড়া, H. *n.* A worm, any creeping thing.

কীমৎ, A. *n.* Price, value, worth.

কীমতী, A. *adj.* Precious, valuable.

কুওৎ, A. *n.* Power, vigour.

কুছ, H. *adj.* Some, any.

কুতুব, A. *n.* Books. (*plu.* of কিতাব).

কুতুবখানা, A. *n.* A library.

কুত্তা, H. *n.* A dog.

কুদরৎ, A. *n.* Power, force; glory; the creation.

কুদরতী, A. *adj.* Powerful, strong, forcible; natural.

কুদরৎওয়ালা, A. *n.* One having power or authority.

কুদ্দুস, A. *adj.* Holy.

রূহ-উল্-কুদ্দুস, the Holy Spirit, আল্-কুদ্দুস, God.

কুন্দা, P. *n.* A piece of wood.

কুফর. A. *n.* Infidelity, blasphemy.

কুফর বকা, A. *v.* To blaspheme.

কুফরাণ, A. *n.* Ingratitude.

কুব্বা, A. *n.* A dome, a cupola, an alcove.

কুমক, P. *n.* Help, assistance; a reinforcement.

কুমক দেওয়া, P. *v.* To help.

কুর্নিশ, P. *n.* Salutation, respect.

কুর্সী, A. *n.* A seat, a chair, a throne; a plinth.

কুর্সীনামা, A. *n.* A genealogy.

কুর্ত্তা, P. *n.* A tunic, a coat.

কুর্ত্তী, P. *n.* A woman's boddice.

কুর্ব্বাণী, A. *n.* Sacrifice.

কুর্ব্বাণী করা, A. *v.* To sacrifice.

কুল, A. *adj.* All, entire, whole.

কুলী, T. A porter, a coolie, a labourer.

কুলু (H. কুলহু) *n.* An oil-press; one who uses an oil-press.

কুলুপ, (A. কুফল). *n.* A lock, a padlock.

কুশ্‌তী, P. *n.* Wrestling.

কুশ্‌তীবাজ, P. *n.* A wrestler.

কুশ্‌তী করা, P. *v.* To wrestle.

কুশাদা, P. *adj.* Open, spacious.

কুণ্ডা, H. *n.* An offering made to a saint.

কুস, A. *n.* A bow.

কেচ্ছা—*See* কিস্‌সা.

কেতা, A. *n.* Arrangement; fashion, mode. (*See* কিতা).

কেতাব—*See* কিতাব,

কেদারা, A. *n.* A couch, a sofa, an easy chair.

কেব্‌লা—*See* কিব্‌লা.

কেয়ামৎ—*See* কিয়ামৎ.

কেরাণী, H. *n.* A clerk. (Probably from the Portuguese.)

কেরাণীখানা, H. *n.* An office.

কেরাণীগিরী, H. *n.* The work of a clerk; a clerkship.

কেরামৎ—*See* করামৎ.

কেরায়া, A. *n.* Hire, rent.

কেরায়াদার, A. *n.* One who hires, a tenant.

কেরায়ানামা, A *n.* A lease.

কের্দ্দানী, P. *n.* Skill, ability

কেল্লা, (A. কল্য়া) *n.* A fort.

কেল্লাদার, A. *n.* The governor of a fortress.

কৈফ, A. *n.* An intoxicating drug.

কৈফীয়ৎ, A. *n.* An explanation, an account, a statement, particulars.

কৈফীয়ৎ দেওয়া, A. *v.* To make a statement, to offer an explanation, to give a report.

কোৎওয়াল, P. *n.* An officer in charge of city police ; a watchman.

কোৎওয়ালী, P. *n.* The office of a *kotwal* ; the principal police station of a city.

কোতাকদ, P. *adj.* Of short stature.

কোতাহী, P. *n.* Shortness ; want poverty.

কোদক, P. *n.* A boy, a youth. (Often written কোদা.)

কোমর—*See* কমর.

কোয়াল, A. *n.* A Muhammadan musician who both sings and plays.

কোয়ালী, A. *n.* The songs sung by a *kouwal*.

কোর্‌ফা, P. *n.* The lease of an undertenant. (Often written কোরপা.)

কোর্‌ফা প্রজা, A tenure-holder under a *Jotdar* a sub-tenant, who holds no permanent right in the land. [a sub-lease.

কোর্‌ফা জমী, P. *n.* Land held under

কোর্‌বাণ—*See* কুর্ব্বাণী.

কোরাণ, A. *n.* The Quran ; the Muhammadan scriptures. (Sometimes written কুরআণ).

কোশাদা—*See* কুশাদা.

কোশিশ, P. *n.* Attempt, trial.

কৌম, A. *n.* A nation, tribe, people.

কৌল, A. *n.* A word ; a promise, an agreement.

কৌসর, A. *n.* A fountain or river in Paradise.

ক্রোক, A. *n.* Distraint of goods ; confiscation, attachment.

ক্রোক করা, A. *v.* To distrain, to seize.

ক্রোকদার, A. *n.* A bailiff : one who distrains property for debt.

ক্রোকী পরওয়ানা, A. *n.* A distraint warrant.

ক্রোক আমীন, A. *n.* An officer of the court who attaches property.

ক্রোক খালাস A. *n.* Release of attachment.

ক্রোক মহল,, A. *n.* An estate under attachment.

খ

খওয়ায়েশ—*See* খোয়াহেশ.

খওয়াব—*See* খুয়াব.

খজল, A. *n.* Shame.

খঞ্জর, A. *n.* A dagger.

খৎ, A. *n.* Handwriting ; a letter ; a bond · a promissory note ; a deed of mortgage.

খৎ-কবালা, A. *n.* A deed of mortgage.

খৎকা, P. *n.* A club, a stick.

খৎনা, A. *n.* Circumcision.

খৎনা করা, A. *v.* To circumcise.

খতব. A. *n.* Betrothing, contracting a marriage.

খৎবা—*See* খুৎবা.

খতম, A. *n.* The end, conclusion; a sealing; the perusal of the Quran from beginning to end.

খতমী, A. *adj.* Last, final.

খতর, (A. খতরা), A. *n.* Danger, risk.

খতী, A. *n.* A mortgagee, *adj.* Mortgaged.

খতা, A. *n.* A sin; a slip, an oversight.

খতান, A. *n.* A calculation, an audit, a reckoning.

খতানন্দ, A. *adj.* sinful.

খতীব, A. *n.* A mosque preacher.

খতীয়ান, A. *n.* A zemindari document containing a detailed statement of a tenant's holding; a ledger; an account-book.

খতীয়ান করা, A. *v.* To make up the ledger; to balance an account.

খদ্দের—*See* খরীদ্দার.

খন্নাস, A. *n.* The devil; a wicked person.

খন্দ, *n.* A crop; a harvest.

খন্দক, A. *n.* A ditch, a moat.

খন্দকার, A. *n.* A Muslim surname.

খফা, P. *adj.* Angry, exasperated.

খফীফ, A. *n.* Disdain, contempt. *adj.* Light, trivial petty.

খবর, A. *n.* News, intelligence; care; the predicate of a sentence.

খবরগীর, A. *n.* A reporter; an informer; a guardian.

খবরগীরী, A. *n.* Protection, guardianship.

খবরের কাগজ, A. *n.* A newspaper.

খবরদার, P. *Int.* Take care! beware!

খবরদারী, P. *n.* Care, watchfulness.

খবীর, A. *adj.* Wise, knowing.

খবীস, A. *adj.* Impure, wicked. *n.* An evil spirit; a miser.

খম, P. *n.* A bend, a twist a curve, a fold. *adj.* Twisted.

খমক, P. *n.* A musical instrument.

খমদার, P. *adj.* Curved, twisted.

খমর, A. *n.* Wine.

খমীর, A. *n.* Leaven. *adj.* Fermented.

খয়র, A. *adj.* Good; lucky, *n.* Well-being, prosperity, health.

খয়র-খোয়া, A. *n.* A well-wisher; a flatterer.

খয়রাৎ, A. *n.* Alms; charity: almsgiving.

খয়রাতী, A. *adj.* Charitable.

খয়রাৎ দেওয়া, A. *v.* To give alms.

খরগোশ, P. *n.* A hare, a rabbit.

খরচ, P. *n.* Expenditure, expense; the debit side of an account.

খরচ করা, P. *v.* To spend; to invest: to cost; to exhaust.

খরচ হওয়া, P. *v.* To be exhausted, to fail.

খরচপত্র, P. *n.* Expenses.

খরচা, P. *n.* Costs, expenses.

খরচা করা, P. *v.* To incur expense.

খরচদার, P. *n.* One who spends.

খরচী. P. *adj.* Extravagant.

খরাজ, A. *n.* Tribute, tax, revenue.

খরাব, A. *adj.* Bad, evil, spoiled.

খরাবী, A. *n.* Evil, badness; difficulty.

খরাব করা, A. *v.* To spoil, to ruin; to taint, to waste. খুন-খরাবী, murder, bloodshed.

খরীতা A. *n.* A letter: a letter-bag *esp.* a silk bag in which letters for great men are enclosed.

খরীদ, P. *n.* A purchase. *adj.* Bought, purchased.

খরীদ করা, P. *v.* To buy.

খরীদগী, P. *n.* A purchase.

খরীদা, P. *adj.* Purchased, bought.

খরীদদার, P. *n.* A purchaser, a consumer.

খরীদ ফরোখৎ, P. *n.* Buying and selling; trade.

খরীফ, A. *n.* The autumn; the autumnal harvest.

খরীফী, A. *adj.* Autumnal.

খর্চ্চা—*See* খরচ.

খল্ক, A. *n.* Creation.

খলীফা, A. *n.* *Khalif;* a successor of Muhammad; the spiritual head of the Muslim world.

খলীফৎ, A. *n.* The office of *Khalif;* spiritual sovereignty over the Muslim world.

খশখাশ, P. *n.* The poppy seed.

খসড়া, (A. খসরা), *n.* A draft, a rough copy; an uncertified copy; a field-book compiled at the time of a land survey; খসড়া বহি, a day-book.

খসম, A. *n.* A husband: a master an owner. [disposition

খসলৎ, A. *n.* Nature, constitution

খাউফ—*See* খৌফ.

খাওন্দ, P. *n.* Lord, husband. (Also written খাবিন্দ.)

খাক, P. *n.* Earth, dust, ashes.

খাকসার, P. *Int.* Your humble petitioner. *adj.* Most humble.

খাকসারী. P. *n.* Self-abasement, humility.

খাকী, P. *adj.* Dusty, earthy; brown: *khaki.*

খাঞ্চা. P. *n.* A tray, a dish.

খাঞ্চাপোশ, P. *n.* A covering for a tray or dish.

খাজা—*See* খাজা.

খাজানা, (A. খজানা) *n.* A treasury; a store; rent, revenue.

খাজাঞ্চী, (A. খজাঞ্চী) *n.* A treasurer, a cashier; a pay-master.

খাজাঞ্চীখানা, A. *n.* A treasury.

খাতক, A. *n.* A debtor; one who borrows money; one who executes any deed of mortgage or promissory note.

খাতকী, A. *adj.* Relating to debtors.

খাতকী কারবার, A. *n.* A money-lending business.

খাতা A. খৎ) *n.* A note-book, an account-book; a party. A plot of land. *See* also under খতা.

খাতা-বহি, A. *n.* A note-book.

খাতা-পত্র, A. *n.* Account books; papers and documents.

খাতিম, A. *n.* A seal-ring; the end.

খাতিমা, A. *n.* End. conclusion; death.

খাতির, A. *n.* Regard, esteem, respect; mind; heart.

খাতির করা, A. *v.* To please, to pay attention to, to show partiality towards ; to indulge.

খাতির খাওয়া, A. *adj.* Desired, approved.

খাতিরজমা, A. *n.* Assurance, satisfaction ; tranquility, composure. *adj.* Contented, tranquil.

খাতিরদার, A. *adj.* Giving encouragement ; showing respect.

খাতিরদারী, A. *n.* Entertainment, hospitality.

খাতির নাদারদ, A. *n.* Disregard, inattention.

খাতুন, T. *n.* A lady, a matron ; Madam : (a common termination of Muslim female names.)

খাদেম, A. *n.* A servant, an attendant ; one in charge of a Muhammadan shrine or religious endowment.

খান, P. *n.* A title of a Persian nobleman ; a headman. খান বাহাদুর, A title of honour bestowed by the British Government in India.

খান্‌কী, P. *n.* A prostitute, a harlot.

খান্‌কীপনা, P. *n.* Prostitution, fornication.

খান্‌কীবাজ, P. *n.* A whoremonger.

খান্‌কীবাজী, P. *n.* Whoredom, prostitution.

খান্‌কীমী, P. *n.* Whoredom.

খান্দান, P. *n.* Lineage, dynasty, family.

খান্দানী, P. *adj.* Ancestral, hereditary.

খান্‌সামা, P. *n.* A house-steward, a butler.

খান্‌সামাগিরী, P. *n.* The work or occupation of a *Khansama*.

খানা, P. *n.* A house, a dwelling ; a receptacle, a place. Dinner, food. (Used much in compounds), as কিতাবখানা, a bookshop.

খানাখরাব, P. *adj.* Ruined, spoiled.

খানাজাদ, P. *n.* A home-born slave.

খানা-তল্লাশ, P. *n.* A house-search.

খানাপিনা, P. *n.* Food and drink.

খানাপুরী, P. *n.* Filling up a column or form.

খানাবাড়ী, P. *n.* A homestead.

খানাশুমারী, P. *n.* House-numbering, a census.

খাপ, P. *n.* A scabbard, a sheath.

খাপছাড়া, P. *adj.* Out of its sheath ; out of place, irrelevant, disconnected.

খাপা, (P. খফা) *adj.* Angry, enraged, excited. (Often written খেপা.)

খাবন্দ, (P. খাওন্দ), *n.* Husband ; master, lord.

খাম, P. *adj.* Raw, imperfect, immature ; gross (not net.)

খাম্‌খা, P. *adv.* Suddenly, unexpectedly.

খাম-খেয়াল, P. *n.* A crude notion, an impracticable idea, a whim.

খাম-খেয়ালী, P. *adj.* Capricious, whimsical, having crude notions.

খামার, *n.* Land in the occupation of the owner and not let out to tenants. *adj.* Non-tenanted.

খামিন্দ—*See* খাওয়ন্দ.

খামী, P. *n.* Imperfection, immaturity; a defect (*esp.* in a title-deed).

খামীরা, A. *n.* Seasoned tobacco.

খামুশ, P. *adj.* Silent.

খামুশী P. *n.* Silence.

খারাব,—*See* খরাব.

খারিজী, A. *n.* A seceder, a schismatic; the name of a Muhammadan sect.

খারেজ, A. *adj.* Excluded, expelled, struck off (a roll).

খারেজ করা, A. *v.* To put outside, to throw out; to except; to reject; to strike off a name from a roll.

খারেজ দাখেল করা, A. *v.* To transfer a property from one tenant to another; to alter the name on the tenant's roll: to dismiss from service.

খারেজা তালুক, A. *n.* A *taluk*, the rents of which are paid direct to Government.

খালা, A. *n.* A maternal aunt, a mother's sister. [liberation.

খালাস, (A খলাস), *n.* Release,

খালাস-পত্র, A. *n.* A passport, an order of release.

খালাসী, A. *n.* An Indian sailor.

খালিসা, A. *n.* Lands under the direct management of the Government: crown lands.

খালী, A. *adj.* Vacant, void, empty. *adj.* Only, alone.

খালু, A. *n.* A maternal uncle; mother's sister's husband.

খালেক, A. *n.* The Creator.

খাস, A. *adj.* Own, private; special, peculiar; select, excellent. (Opposite of আম general.)

খাস আপীল, A. *n.* A special appeal.

খাস মহল, A. *n.* An estate under public management.

খাস কামরা, A. *n.* A private office.

খাস-খামার, A. *n.* Land in the immediate possession of the proprietor, and not let to sub-tenants.

খাস-জমীন, A. *n.* Land the rent of which is taken by Government direct from the tenants.

খাস তহসীল, A. *n.* Government collections of rent direct from the tenants and not through a zemindar or other intermediary.

খাস তালুক, A. *n.* An estate managed by Government.

খাস দখল, A. *n.* Taking actual possession.

খাস নবীস, A. *n.* A private secretary.

খাসবরদার, A. *n.* A personal attendant carrying firearms.

খাসা, A. *adj.* Fine, excellent, tasty. *n.* Disposition, habit.

খাসী, A. *n.* A castrated goat or cock. *adj.* Castrated.

খাসী করা, A v. To castrate; to cut the tap root of a tree.

খাসীয়ৎ, A. n. Peculiarity, natural disposition; attribute.

খাস্তাবাকী, A. n. Balance of rent due by a tenant after a portion has been realized by sale of the estate.

খাহেশ—*See* খোয়াহেশ.

খিড়কী, H. n. A window, a back door. *esp.* A window with shutters. *adj.* Back, private.

খিজর, A. n. The name of a Muhammadan prophet *Khidr.* Elias (?)

খিজালৎ, A. n Shame.

খিতাব, A n. A title, an honorary name.

খিতাব করা, A. v. To address, to speak to.

খিদমৎ, A n. Service, attendance.

খিদমৎ করা. A. v. To serve.

খিদ্মৎগার, A. n. A servant who waits at table. *Khitmagar.*

খিদ্মৎগারী, A. n. The work of a *khitmagar.*

খিমা, A. n. A tent, a pavilion.

খিয়ানৎ, A. n. Perfidy, treachery; loss.

খিয়ার, A. n. Option, selection.

খিয়াল—*See* খেয়াল.

খিরাজ, A. n. Rent, taxes, revenue.

খিরাজ জমী, A. n. Land on which rent is payable.

খিরাজী, A. n. Taxable.

খিল জমী, A. n. Fallow land fit for cultivation.

খিলাৎ, A. n. A robe of honour bestowed on anyone by a superior.

খিলাফ—*See* খেলাফ.

খিসারৎ, A. n. Damage, loss, injury.

খিসারতী, A. *adj.* Harmful, injurious.

খুৎবা, A. n. A sermon delivered at the Friday Muslim prayer and including prayers for the ruling Khalif.

খুদ—*See* খোদ.

খুন, (A খূন). n. Blood, murder.

খুন করা, A. v. To murder.

খুনখরাব, A. n. Murder, bloodshed.

খুনাখুনী, A. n. Murder, bloodshed.

খুনী, A. n. A murderer. *adj.* Murderous, relating to murder; bloody.

খুনজারী, A. n. The shedding of blood; an issue of blood.

খুলা, A. n. A form of Muhammadan divorce at the instance of the woman.

খুলাসা—*See* খোলাসা.

খুনসড়ী, A. n. A quarrel.

খুব, P. *adj.* Good, beautiful, excellent. *adv.* Very, well, much.

খুবসুরৎ, P. *adj.* Beautiful.

খুবানী, P. n. An apricot.

খুবী, P. n. Goodness, beauty.

খুয়াজা, T. n. A title of address to men of position, Sir.

খুয়াব, Also খোয়াব. P. n. A dream; sleep.

খুয়াব দেখা, P. v. To dream.

খুর্মা, P. n. A date tree; a date.

খুশ, P. *n.* Joy, pleasure. *adj.* Good, pleasant; happy.

খুশ্‌কবালা, A. *n.* A registered document under which all rights in certain property are absolutely sold; a voluntary transfer of property.

খুশক, P. *adj.* Dry; bare.

খুশ্‌কী, P. *n.* Dryness; on foot; by land.

খুশখবর, P. *n.* Good news; the Gospel.

খুশজবান, P. *adj.* Eloquent.

খুশনবীস, P. *n.* One who writes well.

খুশনমা, P. *adj.* Pretty, neat, beautiful.

খুশনাম, P. *n.* A good reputation.

খুশমেজাজ, P. *adj.* Happy, contented: jocular.

খুশবো, P. *n.* Fragrance, scent, perfume; incense.

খুশবোগাহ, P. *n.* Alter of incense.

খুশহাল, P. *adj.* Happy, in easy circumstances.

খুশামদ, P. *n.* Adulation, flattery.

খুশামদী, P. *n.* A flatterer.

খুশী, P. *n.* Happiness, joy. *adj.* Happy, pleased.

খেজালৎ—*See* খিজালৎ.

খেতাব—*See* খিতাব.

খেপা, (P. খফা), *adj.* Angry, enraged; mad.

খেয়াল, A. *n.* Thought, imagination; whim, conceit.

খেয়ালী, A. *adj.* Fanciful, imaginary, fantastical; capricious.

খেয়াল করা, A. *v.* To think, to imagine, to consider.

খেরাজ—*See* খিরাজ.

খেলাৎ—*See* খিলাৎ.

খেলাফ, A. *adj.* Against, contrary to; contradictory.
n. Opposition, violation.

খেলাফ করা, A. *v.* To oppose, to violate, to contravene.

খেলাফৎ, A. *n.* *Khalifate;* deputyship; the office of *Khalif*, or spiritual head of the Muhammadan world.

খেসারৎ—*See* খিসারৎ.

খোজা, P. *n.* An eunuch.

খোজখবর, A. *n.* News, information.

খোদ, P. *adj.* Own; private. *n.* Self. *adj.* Personally.

খোদকশ্‌তা জমী, P. *n.* Land cultivated directly by the owner.

খোদকশ্‌তা রাইয়ৎ, P. *n.* A farmer who lives on the land he cultivates; a resident cultivator.

খোদহাকিমী, P. *n.* Self-government; arrogated authority.

খোদা, P. *n.* The Supreme God; *Khuda.*

খোদাবন্দ, P. *n.* Lord, Master.

খোদাবন্দী, P. *n.* Lordship.

খোদাই, P. *n.* Godhead, divinity.

খোদাপরস্ত, P. *adj.* God-fearing, pious.

খোন্‌কার, P. *n.* A Muhammadan who performs the operation of circumcision.

খোয়াব, P. *n.* A dream.

খোয়ার, P. *n.* Corruption. *adj.* Evil.

খোয়াই, P. *n.* Wishing, desiring.

খোয়াহেশ, P. *n.* Wish, desire.

খোর P. A suffix signifying being addicted to, eating, drinking. using etc as মদ-খোর, one addicted to strong drink.

খোরপোশ, P. *n.* Food and raiment.

খোরাক, P. *n.* Food, provisions: rations, diet.

খোরাকী. P. *n.* Subsistence money, board, a daily allowance of food or money.

খোলাসা, A. *n.* An abstract, the substance of a thing. *adj.* Clear, manifest; loose; free. *adv.* Freely; clearly; sincerely.

খোলাসা করা, A *v.* To make clear; to liberate

খোশ—*See* খুশ.

খোসাল—*See* খুশহাল.

খৌফ, A. *n.* Fear.

খ্যাতনামা, P. *adj.* Famous.

গা

গওয়াহ, P. *n.* A witness.

গওয়াহী. P. *n.* Testimony, evidence, witness.

গওয়াহী দেওয়া, P. *n.* To give testimony.

গজ, P. *n.* A yard; a foot-rule; a ram-rod, an iron bar. (Sometimes written গোজ.)

গজব, A. *n.* Anger; vengeance. *adj.* Angry, displeased; wonderful, unique. (Often written গুজব)

গজব করা, A. *v.* To be angry; to work wonders, to cause surprise.

গজরনা, P. *v.* To pass, to elapse (time); to die.

গজল, A. *n.* An ode, a hymn.

গজন্তা—*See* গুজশ্‌তা,

গণ্ডা, H. *n.* A bad character a rascal, a bully.

গণ্ডামী, H. *n.* Knavery, rascality.

গঞ্জ, P. *n.* A market.

গঞ্জীয়া, P. *n.* A bag, a purse, a wallet.

গঞ্জীফা. P. *n.* Cards for playing.

গতখামার, P. *n.* Land taken out from খাস-খামার.

গতরাইয়তী জমী, A. *n.* Land surrendered by a tenant to the zemindar.

গদী, P. *n.* A cushion, a seat, a bench, a throne.

গদর, P. *n.* A riot; disorder, rebellion.

গদীয়ান, P. *n.* A banker, a merchant.

গদীর, A. *n.* A Shiah festival when images of Abu Bakr, Omar and Othman are desecrated.

গন্দম, P. *n.* Wheat.

গনী, A. *n.* A rich person. *adj.* Rich.

আল্-গনী, a name of God.

গপ P. *n.* Tattle, gossip, idle talk.

গফর, A *n.* Forgiveness.

গফ্ফার, A. *adj.* Forgiving. *n.* One who forgives.

আল্-গফফার, a name of God.

গফ্লৎ, A. *n.* Inattention, remissness, carelessness.

গফুর, A. *adj.* Forgiving. *n.* আল্-গফুর a name of God.

গবাহ—See গওয়াহ.

গম, P. A. *adj.* Missing, distracted; concealed; sorrowful. *n.* Mourning, sorrow:

গম্‌গীন, P. *adj.* Sorrowful, depressed.

গম্‌রাহ. P. *adj.* Erring, wandering; led astray.

গম্‌রাহ করা, P. *v.* To lead astray.

গয়রহ্, A. And the rest, *et cetera.*

গয়েন্দা—See গোয়েন্দা.

গর—See গৈর

গরক, A. *n.* A drowning, a sinking. *adj.* Immersed, absorbed in; drowned.

গরজ, A. *n.* A wish, desire; object; self-interest; urgency.

গরজী, A. *adj.* Self-interested, selfish; urgent.

গরদ, P. *n.* Dust. (Also written গরদা.)

গরদখোর, P. *adj.* Filthy, dirty.

গরদন, P. *n.* The neck; the head.

গরদন মারা, P. *v.* To behead.

গরদান, P. *n.* A turning, a revolving.

গরদিশ, P. *n.* Revolution; adverse fortune.

গরদুন, P. *n.* The heavens.

গরব, P. *n.* The west.

গরম, P. *adj.* Warm; glowing; angry.

গরমী. P. *n.* Heat, warmth; passion.

গরমিল—See গৈরমিল.

গরম-মেজাজ, P. *adj.* Hot-headed, passionate.

গরীব, A. *adj.* Poor, destitute; needy; humble.

গরীবদেল A. *adj.* Meek.

গরীবানা, A. *adj.* Humble. *n.* Humble behaviour.

গরীবী, A. *n.* Poverty, want; humility.

গরুব—See গুরুব.

গলৎ, A. *adj.* Wrong, incorrect, false.

গলতী, A. *n.* A mistake, an error; a fallacy.

গল্‌বা, A. *n.* Superiority, supremacy; ascendancy.

গলাবন্দ, (P. গুলুবন্দ.) *n.* A necklace; a comforter worn on the neck.

গলীজ, A. *adj.* Thick; filthy, dirty.

গশৎ, P. *n.* A walking about.

গশ্‌তিদার, P. *n.* One who travels about to purchase in the cheapest markets. (Often written গস্তিদার.)

গস্তানী, P. *n.* A prostitute. *adj.* Whorish, licentious.

গহরা, H. *adj.* Deep; profound; strong (liquor).

গাজী, A. *n.* A warrior; a Muslim who fights in a religious war; a *ghazi.*

গারোয়ান, (H. গাড়ীবান). *n.* A coachman, a cabman; a carter.

গাফের,, A. *adj.* Forgiving.

গাফেল, A. *adj.* Indolent, careless, negligent.

গাফেলী, A. *n.* Indolence, carelessness.

গাফলৎ, (A. গফ্‌লৎ). *n.* Indolence, carelessness.

গায়েব, A. *adj.* Hidden, secret; invisible.

গায়েবী, A. *n.* Invisibility.
গায়েবৎ, A. *n.* Invisibility ; absence.
গায়ের—*See* গৈর.
গার, P. *n.* A suffix denoting the doer, or agent as খিদ্‌মৎগার, one who serves.
গারৎ, A. *n.* Plunder ; destruction.
গারী, P. *n.* A suffix denoting doing or making, as খিদ্‌মৎগারী, the doing service *i.e.* the occupation of one who serves.
গার, A. *n.* Plunder, robbery.
গালিচা, P. *n.* A carpet, a rug.
গালেব, A. *adj.* Overcoming, surpassing, victorious, excelling.
গাহ্, P. A suffix denoting time or place as, এবাদৎগাহ্, a place of worship, a temple.
গাহেন, H. *n.* A hymn, a song.
গিরদ, P. *adj.* Surrounding, around. *See* গির্‌দাহ্.
গির্‌দাহ্, P. *n.* A round pillow ; a shield ; a circle. (Often written গিরদ.)
গিরদওয়ার, P. *adj.* Circular.
গিরা, H. *v.* To fall.
গিরী, P. A suffix denoting the work, functions or occupation of the agent, as কেরাণীগিরী, the occupation of a clerk.
গিলা, P. *n.* A complaint.
গিলা করা, P. *v.* To complain. (Sometimes written গিল্লা.)
গিলাগুজার, P. *adj.* Censorious ; abusive.
গিলাফ, A. *n.* A case, a quilt ; *Esp.* the cloth covering of the *Kaaba* at Mecca.
গীন, P. A suffix denoting full of, possessed by &c. as গম্‌গীন, full of sorrow *i.e.* sorrowful.
গীর, P. A suffix denoting taking, seizing etc. [গজব.
গুজব, A. *n.* A rumour. *See* under
গুজর, P. *n.* A passage, a road.
গুজরান্, P. *n.* A passing by, a going ; a livelihood. *adj.* Spent, gone, passed.
গুজরিয়া যাওয়া, P. *v.* To pass away.
গুজশ্‌তা, P. *adj.* Elapsed, past, previous ; remitted.
গুজার, P. *n.* One who gives or pays over to another.

মাল-গুজার, One who pays Government revenue.

মাল-গুজারী, Payment of Government revenue.

গুজারা, P. *n.* A ferry-boat.
গুজারৎ, P. *adv.* Through the medium of, by, by means of.
গুজারৎ-খোদ, P. By oneself, per self.
গুজারিশ, P. *n.* Payment ; transfer.
গুদড়, H. *n.* Rubbish ; old rags or papers.
গুন্‌জায়েশ, P. *n.* Capacity, contents ; advantage.
গুন্‌জায়েশী, P. *adj.* Advantageous.
গুনাহ, P. *n.* Sin, fault. (Often written গোনা.)
গুনাহ্‌গার, P. *n.* A sinner.
গুনাহ্‌গারী, P *n.* Sin.
গুম্বজ, P. *n.* A vault, an arch, a dome ; a turret.
গুমরাহ—*See* গম্‌রাহ.
গুমান, P. *n.* Pride, haughtiness ; fancy, doubt, suspicion.

গুমান করা, P. *v.* To imagine, to fancy ; to suspect.

গুমানী, P. *adj.* Suspicious, fanciful ; proud, conceited.

গুমশ্‌তহ—*See* গোমস্তা.

গুনাহ—*See* গওনাহ.

গুরূর, A. *n.* Pride.

গুল, P. *n.* A flower ; a rose ; smoked tobacco.

গুলজার, P. *n.* A garden. *adj.* Beautiful, grand, splendid.

গুলগুল, P. *n.* Noise, report ; rumour.

গুলতরাশ, P. *n.* A maker of artificial flowers.

গুলান, (?) *n.* An arrangement for payment of rent by a stipulated portion of the crop.

গুসল, A. *n.* Bathing purification by water.

গুসল করা, A. *v.* To bathe.

গুসলখানা, A. *n.* A bath-room.

গেঁজিয়া, H. *n.* A purse, a bag.

গেরদ—*See* গিরদ.

গেরাণ, P. *adj.* Dear, costly.

গেরাণী, P. *n.* Dearness, scarcity.

গেরাফী, *n.* An anchor.

গেরেফতার, P. *adj.* Seized, arrested ; involved, entangled.

গেরেফতার করা, *v.* To arrest, to seize.

গেরেফতারী, P. *n.* Seizure. arrest ; imprisonment.

গৈর, P. A prefix signifying except, without, absent, different from, lack of, etc.

গৈর-আসল, *adj.* Not genuine, unreal.

গৈর-ইনসাফ, *n.* An injustice.

গৈর-কাবেল, *adj.* Unfit for, unable.

গৈর-খিরাজ, , *n.* Rent-free land.

গৈর-জব্দ, *adj.* Omitted, excepted ; rent free.

গৈর-তকসীর, *adj.* Faultless, innocent.

গৈর-তদবীর, *n.* Carelessness.

গৈর-পসন্দ, *n.* Disapproval, dislike.

গৈর-মনকুলা, *n.* Immovable property.

গৈর-মশরুৎ, *adj.* Unconditional.

গৈর-মিল, *n.* Discrepancy, disagreement.

গৈর-রাজী, *adj.* Unwilling.

গৈর-লায়েক, *adj.* Unworthy.

গৈর-সাকিন, *adj.* Non-resident.

গৈর-সিলসিলা, *adj.* Irregular, summary.

গৈর-হাজির, *adj.* Absent.

গোতা, A. *n.* A dip, a dive.

গোঁয়ার, H. *n.* A villager, a rustic ; a boor, a churl. *adj.* Boorish churlish ; stupid.

গোজ, A. *n.* Talk, gossip.

গোনা—*See* গুনাহ্‌.

গোমরা—*See* গমরাহ.

গোমস্তা, (P. গুমাশ্‌তহ্‌.) *n.* An agent ; a rent-collector ; a zemindary officer.

গোয়েন্দা, P. *n.* An informer, a spy, a detective.

গোয়েন্দাগিরী, , P. *n.* The business or work of a detective or spy.

গোর, P. *n.* A grave, a tomb.

গোর দেওয়া, P. *v.* To bury.

গোরস্থান, P. *n.* A cemetary, a graveyard.

গোর কফান, P. *n.* Funeral ceremonies. *adj.* White, fair.

গোরা, P. *n.* A European soldier.

গোল, P. *n.* Noise. uproar.

গোলাব, P. *n.* A rose; rose-water. (Also written গোলাপ.)

গোলাম A. *n.* A slave; a boy.

গোলামী, P. *n.* Slavery, bondage.

গোলন্দাজ, H. *n.* A gunner: artillery.

গোলন্দাজী, P. *n.* Gunnery.

গোশওয়ারা, P. *n.* An abstract of accounts; an ear-ring.

গোশ্‌ত্‌, P. *n.* Meat, flesh.

গোশা, P. *n.* Retirement, privacy; a secluded spot.

গোশা-নশীন, P. *adj.* Retired, secluded. *n.* A Muhammadan ascetic; a women kept in seclusion.

গোস—*See* গোস্ত.

গোস্তাখ, P. *adj.* Impudent, audacious.

গোস্তাখী, P. *n.* Impudence; contempt, audacity.

গোসল—*See* গুসল.

গোসসা, A. *n.* Anger; grief. *adj.* Angry, grieved.

গোহরী, P. *n.* A process-fee; an extra fee for delay, demurrage.

গৌস. A. *n.* A title of certain Muhammadan saints.

গ্রেফতার—*See* গেরেফতার.

ঘ

ঘবরান, H. *v.* To be confused, to be perplexed.

ঘবরাহৎ, H. *n.* Confusion, perplexity, agitation.

ঘরাণা, H. *n.* Lineage, dynasty, family members.

ঘোজ, H. *n.* A small plot of land the boundaries of which are not straight.

চ

চক, H. *n.* A portion of a zemindari.

চকবন্দী, P. *n.* The dividing of land into plots; the delimitation of the boundaries of land; the boundaries of a police or revenue jurisdiction.

চকলা, P. A district, a division of country; a quarter of a town; an estate.

চকলাদার, P. The head of a district, the holder of an estate.

চকলী, P. *n.* A pulley over a well in which the rope runs.

চপরাস, P. *n.* A plate or badge worn by a peon.

চপরাসী, P. *n.* A peon, a court messenger. (Often written চাপরাসী.)

চবুতা, H. *n.* A raised terrace, a platform; a police-station.

চরখা, P. *n.* A spinning-wheel.

চরপুজ, P. *adj.* Weak, feeble; foolish.

চরেন্দা, P. *n.* An animal that grazes.

চর্ব্বী, P. *n.* Fat, tallow, suet.

চর্ব্বীদার, P. *adj.* Greasy.

চশম. P. *n.* The eye; a fountain.

চশমখোর, P. *adj.* Seeing nothing, purblind

চশমখোরী, P. *n.* The state of being wilfully blind.

চশমা, P. *n.* Spectacles; a fountain, a spring.

চাঁদা, P. *n.* A contribution, collection, an assessment.

চাঁদী, H. *n.* Silver.

চাক, P. *n.* A split, a rent.

চাকর, P. *n.* A domestic servant.

চাকরা, P. *n.* Land given free of rent for services rendered; land given in lieu of wages.

চাকরাণ, P. *adj.* Feudal.

চাকরাণা, P. *n.* A fee; a gift of land for services rendered, lands exempt from revenue.

চাকরাণী, P. *n.* A female servant.

চাকরী. P. *n.* Service, employment.

চাকরী করা, P. *v.* To serve, to take employment.

চাকলা—*See* চকলা.

চাকু, P. *n.* A pen-knife.

চাচা, H. *n.* An uncle, a father's brother.

চাচী, H. *n.* An aunt, a father's brother's wife.

চাচত ভাই, H. *n.* Cousin, father's brother's son.

চাদর, (P. চদর) *n.* A sheet; a kind of upper garment; a large cloth as table cloth etc.

চাপকান, (P. চপকন) *n.* A long garment worn by Muhammadans.

চাপরাসী—*See* চপরাসী.

চাবুক, P. *n* A whip.

চাবুক মারা, P. *v.* To whip, to scourge.

চামচ, (P. চমচা). *n.* A spoon.

চারপাই, H. *n.* A bedstead, a litter.

চারা, P. *n.* A cure, at remedy, redress.

চালাক, P. *adj.* Active, clever, expert; tricky, artful.

চালাকী, P. *n.* Activity; cleverness; trickery, deception.

চালাকী করা, P. *v.* To trick; to act with cunning; to be skilful.

চাহারম, H. *adj.* Fourth.

চাহারম জমী, Land which only yields one fourth of a normal crop.

চিক, T. *n.* A blind, a screen.

চিকন, P. *adj.* Fine, smooth. *n.* Needlework, embroidery.

চিকনদোজ, P. *n.* An embroiderer.

চিজ,—*See* চীজ.

চিঠা, H. *n* A rough draft; a note; a list; a zemindary document giving measurements of lands.

চিঠী, H. *n.* A letter, a note: a certificate.

চিড়িয়া, H. *n.* A bird.

চিড়িয়াখানা, H. *n.* An aviary.

চিড়িয়ামার, H. *n.* A bird-catcher.

চিরকুট, H. *n.* A note, a slip of paper containing some message.

চিরাগ, P. *n.* A lamp.

চিরাগদান, P. *n.* A lamp-stand.

চিলম, P. *n.* The bowl of an Indian tobacco-pipe.

চিলমচী, T. *n.* A wash-hand basin.

চিল্লানা, H. *v.* To scream, to screech.

চিল্লাচিল্লি, H. *n.* A scream, a screech.

চীজ, P. *n.* A thing, an article.

চীজবস্ত, P. *n.* Goods, furniture

চুগল, P. *n.* A tale-bearer, an informer.

চুগলখোর, P. *n.* A slanderer, a back-biter.

চুগলখোরী, P. *n.* Slander, defamation.

চেহারা, (P. চহরহ্). *n.* Face; image; aspect.

চোক, H. *n.* The main street of a city ; the city square.

চোখা, H. *adj.* Sharp, keen ; genuine.

চোগা, T. *n.* An overcoat; a cloak.

চোব, P. *n.* A stick, a club, a mace.

চোব্‌দার, P. *n.* A mace-bearer. (Sometimes written চোপদার.)

চোস্ত, P. *adj.* Fleet, active. *n.* A stool, a chair.

চৌকী, P. *n.* A police-station ; the beat of a watchman ; a guard, a watch.

চৌকী দেওয়া, P. *v.* To keep watch, to guard.

চৌকীদার, P. *n.* A guard, a watchman.

চৌকীদারী, P. *n.* The occupation of a *chaukidar* : pertaining to a *chaukidar*.

চৌথ, H. *n.* A quarter.

চৌপায়া, P. *n.* A piece of furniture with four legs.

চৌহদ্দী, P. *n.* Boundaries, limits.

চৌহদ্দী করা, P. *v.* To limit, to define.

ছ

ছাওয়াল, *n.* A child, a boy.

ছানী.—*See* সানী.

ছওয়াল—*See* সুয়াল.

ছিতর বিতর করা, H. *v.* To tear in pieces.

ছিন্নি—*See* শিন্নি.

ছুয়াল—*See* সুয়াল.

জ

জওজ—*See* জোজ.

জওয়ান, P. *n.* A youth, a young man. *adj.* Strong, vigorous.

জওয়ানী, P. *n.* Youth, manhood ; puberty.

জওয়াব, A. *n.* A reply ; a dismissal ; a rejoinder ; a defence. (Also written জবাব).

জওয়াব দেওয়া, A. *v.* To dismiss ; to file a statement ; to make a reply.

জওয়াব করা, A. *v.* To answer.

জওয়াবদিহী, A. *n.* Liability, responsibility.

জওয়াবদিহী করা, A. *v.* To contest a claim ; to defend an action.

জওয়াহির,—*See* জোয়াহির

জকশক, A. *adj.* Hard-pressed ; weak.

জকাৎ, A. *n.* Alms ; *Esp.* the legal Muhammadan alms enjoined by the Qurân.

জখম, P. *n.* A wound ; an ulcer.

জখমী, P. *adj.* Wounded.

জজ—*See* জুজ.

জজাক, A. *int.* Bravo !

জজাক-আল্লা, A. *int.* God bless you !

জজীরৎ, A. *n.* An island.

জজীরৎ-উল্-আরব, the Arabian peninsula.

জঙ্গ, P. *n.* War, battle ; rust.

জঙ্গ করা, P. *n.* To make war.

জঙ্গী, P. *adj.* Warlike, military.

জঙ্গী লাট, P. *n.* The military Commander-in-chief in India.

জঞ্জাল, H. *n.* Trouble, difficulty.

জঞ্জীর, P. *n.* A chain. (Sometimes written জিঞ্জীর.)

জঞ্জীরা, P. *n.* A necklace ; chain stitch, herring boning (in tailoring.)

জন্নৎ, A. *n.* A garden; paradise. (Also written জিন্নৎ.)

জন্নতী, A. *adj.* Heavenly.

জনাজা, A. *n.* A bier, a coffin; a corpse.

জনানা, *P. n.* A woman, a female; the female apartments. (Sometimes written জানানা.) *adj.* Female, feminine.

জনানী, P. *adj.* Pertaining to women. feminine.

জনাব, A. *int.* Sir! Your honour!

জনুন—*See* জুনুন.

জন্দ, P. *n.* An army; soldiers.

জফর, A. *n.* Victory, gain.

জফাফ, A. *n.* The first going of a bride to her husband's home, consummation of marriage.

জব, H. *adj.* When, as soon as.

জবৎ, A. *n.* Confiscation, forfeiture; restraint.

জবতক, H. *adj.* Until; as long as.

জবর, A. *n.* Force, coercion, oppression. In Persian it represents the vowel a. *adj.* Strong, great, *adv.* Very; much.

জবর করা, A. *v.* To force, to coerce, to compel.

জবরজুলুম, A. *n.* Oppression, tyranny.

জবরদস্ত, A. *adj.* High-handed; powerful; authoritative.

জবরদস্তী. A. *n.* High-handedness; authority, compulsion, oppression.

জবরদস্তী করা, A. *v.* To use force, to compel; to oppress.

জবরাণ, A. *adv.* By force, forcibly.

জবরদার, Same as জবরদস্ত.

জবল, A. *n.* A mountain.

জবহ্, A. *n.* Sacrifice, slaughter. (Sometimes written জবাই.)

জবহ্ করা, A. *v.* To slaughter, to sacrifice.

জবাই—*See* জবহ. [a language.

জবান, P. *n.* The tongue; a word;

জবানবন্দী, P. *n.* A written deposition; an affidavit.

জবানবন্দী করা, P. *v.* To take down a deposition.

জবানী, P. *adj.* Verbal, oral.

জবাব—*See* জওয়াব. [victorious.

জব্বার, A. *n.* Powerful, strong, আল্-জব্বার, One of the names of God.

জব্দ, A. *n.* Restraint, control. *adj.* Restrained. controlled, subdued.

জব্দ করা, A. *v.* To restrain, to control, to overcome; to humiliate.

জবুর, A. *n.* The *Zaboor*, the Psalms of David. [rust.

জম, A. *n.* Contraction, conjunction;

জম ধরা, A. *n.* To get rusty.

জমজম্, A. *n.* A well at the *Kaaba* in Mecca; a crowd.

জমলা, A. *n.* The whole, total; a heap, a crowd.

জমা, A. *n.* A collection, a sum, total; the credit side of an account; rent payable to a landlord, capital. *adj.* Collected, gathered, assembled.

জমা দেওয়া, A. *v.* To credit an account, to enter on the credit side of an account; to lease out.

জমা হওয়া, A. *v.* To assemble, to come together.

জমা লওয়া, A. *v.* To rent from.

জমা করা, A. *v.* To add, to collect.

জমাই, A. *adj.* Fiscal, financial. *n.* Those who pay rent.

জমা-ওয়াসীল-বাকী, A. *n.* A statement showing payments due for rent, together with the amounts recovered or still in arrears.

জমা-খরচ, A. *n.* Income and expenditure; the credit and debtor sides of an account; a current account.

জমা-গুজশ্‌তা, A. *n.* A statement of rent due for a previous year.

জমাৎ, H. *adj.* Congealed, frozen.

জমাতুমারী, A. *n.* Rent ascertained by personal enquiry of the tenants.

জমাদার, A. *n.* A chief or headman; a head-constable; an Indian subaltern military officer.

জমাদারী, A. *n.* The work or function of a *jamadar*.

জমানৎ, A. *n.* Security, safety; a bail bond. (Sometimes written জামানৎ.)

জমানৎনামা, A. *n.* A written bond.

জমানা, A. *n.* Time, period, an age; the world.

জমাবন্দী, A. *n.* The settlement of the revenues of a province; a written zemindari statement of the tenants, showing the amount of rent to be paid, the area of the holding and other details; assessment.

জমায়েৎ, A. *n.* Collection.: a party, a company; a society; a meeting a congregation a gathering: *Esp.* for prayer in a mosque. (Sometimes written জামাৎ.)

জমায়েৎ হওয়া, A. *v.* To be assembled.

জমাল, A. *n.* Beauty, elegance.

জমালী, A. *adj.* The lovable and merciful attributes of God, as opposed to the জলালী, terrible attributes.

জমী, (P. জমীন). *n.* Land, the earth; arable land.

জমী করা, P. *v.* To buy land for cultivation.

জমীন—*See* জমী.

জমীনী, P. *adj.* Relating to earth; terrestrial; relating to arable lands.

জমীনদার, P. *n.* A land-holder, a *zemindar*. (Often written জমীদার.)

জমীনদারী, P. *n.* An estate, landed property; the occupation or tenure of a *zemindar*. (Often written জমীদারী.)

জমীনদারী পাট্টা, P. *n.* A document granted by Government recognizing the right of a zemindar.

জমীনদারী জমা, P. *n.* The revenue paid to Government by a zemindar.

জমীর, A. *n.* The conscience; the heart.

জমীল, A. *adj.* Beautiful, elegant.

জয়ীফ, A. *adj.* Weak, feeble.

জয়ীফী, A. *n.* Weakness, infirmity

জর, P. *n.* Gold.

জরদস্ত, P. *adj.* Covetous.
জরকশী, P. *adj.* Woven with gold.
জরদ, P. *adj.* Yellow.
জরব, A. *n.* A blow.
জরিমানা, A. *n.* A fine, a penalty.
জরিমানা করা, A. *v.* To fine.
জরিয়া, A. *n.* A medium, means; influence; interest. [through.
জরিয়া সে, A. *adv.* By means of,
জরী, P. *n.* Gold or silver thread.
জরীদা, A. *n.* A register; an account-book.
জরীদার, P. *adj.* Woven with gold or silver thread.
জরীপেশগী, P. *n.* An advance (of money in payment.)
জরীপ, (A. জরীব). *n.* A measurement, a survey.
পরতল জরীপ, A re-survey.
জরীপ করা, A. To measure, to survey.
জরীপ আমীন, A. *n.* A surveyor.
জরীপী, A. *adj.* Relating to surveying.
জরু—*See* জোরু.
জরুর, A. *adj.* Necessary; urgent, indispensable; incumbent.
জরুরী,—Same as জরুর.
জরুরৎ, A. *n.* Necessity; compulsion.
জরুরতী, A. *adj.* Necessary, urgent.
জর্‌রা, A. *n.* A particle, an atom, a little.
জলদ, P. *adj.* Quick, fast.
জল্‌দী, P. *adv.* Quickly.
জলদবাজ, P. *adj.* Quick, active.
জলদবাজী, P. *n.* Quickness.
জল্‌সা, A. *n.* A meeting, an assembly; an entertainment; the sitting posture in Muhammadan liturgical prayer.

জলাল, A. *n.* Majesty, glory; fury. (Often written জালাল).
জলালী, A. *adj.* The 'terrible' attributes of God. (*See* under জমালী.)
জল্লাদ, P. *n.* An executioner.
জল্লাদী, P. *n.* The office of an executioner.
জলীল, A. *adj.* Great, glorious. illustrious.
জলুস—*See* জুলুস.
জশন, P. *n.* Joy, delight.
জশনী, P. *adj.* Joyful.
জহন্নম, A. *n.* Hell.
জহন্নমী, A. *adj.* Hellish, infernal. *n.* The inhabitants of hell.
জহমৎ, A. *n.* Sickness, pain.
জহর, A. *n.* Manifestation, publication. P. *n.* Poison; a flower; beauty. *adj.* Bitter.
জহান, P. *n.* The world. (Often written জাহান.)
জহান পনাহ, P. *n.* A king. *Int.* Your majesty.
জাওজ—*See* জৌজ.
জাইগীর—*See* জাগীর.
জাইদাদ—*See* জায়দাদ.
জাগীর, P. Rent-free gift of land; fief.
জাগীরদার, P. *n.* The holder of a *jagir*.
জাড়া, H. *n.* Cold; the winter.
জাত, P. *n.* Essence; self; nature.
জাতী, P. *adj.* Essential; constitutional.
জাদা, (P. জাদেহ). *n.* A son, a child. (Often used as a suffix, as হারামজাদা, an illegitimate son.)

জাদী, P. *n.* A daughter.

জাদু, P. *n.* Sorcery, divination.

জাদুকর, (P. জাদুগর). *n.* A sorcerer, a diviner.

জাদুকরী. P. *n.* Sorcery.

জাদুঘর, P. *n.* A museum.

জান, P. *n.* Life ; the soul.

জানওয়ার, P. *n.* An animal, a creature.

জান্‌দার, P. *adj.* Active, powerful.

জানপুহ্‌চান, P. *n.* Acquaintance.

জানবাজ, P. *adj.* Spirited, active.

জানানা—*See* জনানা.

জানালা, *n.* A window.

জানী, A. *n.* An adulterer, a fornicator.

জানীয়া, A. *n.* An adulteress.

জানেব, A. *n.* Side, a part. *adv.* Towards.

জানেবদার, A. *n.* A supporter, a defender. *adj.* Biassed, partial.

জানেবদারী, A. *n.* Partiality.

জাফরী, P. *n.* Lattice-work of split bamboos.

জাবেদা, (P. জাবিতহ্) *n.* Custom, a judicial usage ; a law ; a draft ; a rough account-book.

জাবেদা নকল, *n.* An authoritative copy of legal document.

জাবেদা আপীল, P. A legal appeal in regular form.

জামদানী, P. *n.* Cloth in which flowers are woven ; a trunk.

জামা, P. *n.* A coat, a gown ; the principle mosque of a city. A. All ; whole.

জামাওয়ার, P. *n.* A decorated shawl. (Often written জামিয়ার.)

জামাৎ—*See* জমায়েৎ.

জামানৎ—*See* জমায়েৎ.

জামিন, A. *n.* Security, bail, a guarantee.

ফেল্‌-জামিন, A. *n.* A bond binding one down to keep the peace.

মাল-জামিন, A. *n.* Security for payment of money.

হাজির জামিন, A. *n.* Surety for appearing in court.

জামিনী, A. *n.* Suretyship.

জামিনদার, A. *n.* A sponsor ; security.

জামিনদারী, A. *n.* Suretyship, sponsorship.

জামিননামা, A. *n.* A deed by which one undertakes to stand surety for another.

জায়গীর—*See* জাগীর.

জায়, P. *n.* A list, a catalogue ; loss, damage. *adj.* Damaged ; right, proper, just. (For জায়েজ)

জায়গা, P. *n.* A place ; room ; a quarter.

জায়বাকী, A. *n.* The balance of an account.

জায়দাদ, P. *n.* Funds, property ; an estate ; assignment of revenue for the maintenance of an estate.

জায়েজ, A. *adj.* Lawful, permissable, proper, right, just.

জায়েব, *adj.* Settled.

জার, P. *n.* Lamentation, weeping.

জারী, A. *n* A declaration, a manifestation ; currency, circulation ; issue. *adj.* Current, in force ; customary ; flowing.

জারী করা, A. *v.* To proclaim, to publish; to execute, to issue (an order); to pass (a law); to serve (a summons).

জাল, A. *n.* A forgery. *adj.* Forged.

জালসাজ, A. *n.* A forger.

জালাল—*See* জলাল.

জালিয়াৎ, A. *n.* A forger.

জালিয়াতী, A. *n.* A forgery.

জালেম, A. *n.* A tyrant, an oppressor. *adj.* Oppressive, tyrannical.

জাসুস, A. *n.* A spy, an emissary.

জাস্তি, A. *n.* Addition, excess.

জাহান্নম—*See* জহন্নম.

জাহাজ, A. *n.* A ship, a vessel.

জাহাজী, A. *adj.* Nautical, pertaining to a ship. *n.* One working on a ship.

জাহান—*See* জহান.

জাহির, A. *n.* A disclosure; a display, a manifestation. *adj.* Clear, plain, palpable; outward.

জাহির করা, A. *v.* To publish, to disclose.

জাহির হওয়া,, A. *v.* To be clear, to be apparent.

জাহিরী, A. *adj.* Outward, public.

জাহিরা, A. *adv.* Openly, publicly.

জাহেদ, A. *n.* One who fights in a *jehad* or religious war.

জাহেল, A. *adj.* Ignorant.

জিকর, A. *n.* Talk, mention, recital (*Esp.* of the names of God); remembrance.

জিজিয়া, A. *n.* A poll-tax formerly levied by Muslims on Jews and Christians. This later. in India. was extended to Hindus also.

জিদ্, A. *n.* Opposition; obstinancy; importunity.

জিদী. A. *adj.* Obstinate, perverse.

জিঞ্জীর—*See* জঞ্জীর.

জিন্, A. *n.* A demon; a *jinn.*

জিন্নৎ—*See* জন্নৎ.

জিনিস, (A. জিন্স্). *n.* A thing, an article; kind, sort, species; sex; classification.

জিনা, A. *n.* Adultery, fornication.

জিনাকার, A. *n.* An adulterer.

জিনাকারী, A. *n.* Adultery.

জিন্দা, P. *adj.* Alive, living.

জিন্দগী, P. *n.* Life.

জিন্দগীভোর, P. *adv.* For the whole of life.

জিম্মা, A. *n.* Custody, care, charge.

জিম্মাদার, A. *n.* A custodian; a trustee; one in charge.

জিম্মী, A. *n.* One who paid the *jiziya* or poll-tax to the Muhammadans.

জিয়াদা, A. *adj.* Much, more, excessive, many.

জিয়াদতী, A. *n.* Oppression, force; excess.

জিয়াফৎ, A. *n.* A feast, an entertainment.

জিয়ারৎ, A. *n.* The visitation of tombs; pilgrimage.

জিয়ারৎ করা, A. *v.* To visit tombs; to go on pilgrimage.

জিয়ারতী. A. *n.* A pilgrim.

জিরন্দাজ. P. *n.* An ornamental cover for an Indian pipe-stand.

জিরাৎ,—*See* জিরায়ৎ.

জিরায়ৎ, A. *n.* Crops, harvest; land planted with crops. (Sometimes written জিরাৎ).

জিরায়ৎ করা, A. *v.* To cultivate, to till.

জিল্দ, A. *n.* A volume; leather; the binding of a book.

জিল্দ বান্ধা, A. *v.* To bind a book.

জিল্দগর, A. *n.* A book-binder.

জিলা—*See* জেলা.

জিল্লা, A. *n.* Brightness, lustre.

জিল্লাদার, A. *adj.* Bright, shining.

জিসম, A. *n.* The body.

জিসমানী, A. *adj.* Bodily, carnal; material.

জিসমী, A. *adj.* Personal, bodily.

জিহাদ. A. *n.* Muhammadan religious war. *Jehad.*

জীন, P. *n.* A saddle.

জীনৎ, A. *n.* Beauty, elegance; an ornament.

জীনপোশ, P. *n.* A saddle-cloth.

জীনা, P. *n.* A ladder, stairs.

জীব, A. *n.* A pocket. (Sometimes written জেব.)

জীবী, A. *adj.* Belonging to the pocket, relating to the pocket.

জীরা, P. *n.* Cummin-seed; pollen.

জুজ, A. *n.* Portion, part; volume.

জুজবন্দী, A. *n.* Book-binding.

জুদা, P. *adj.* Separate, distinct, different.

জুদাই, P. *n.* Separation; difference.

জুনুন, A. *n.* Madness, lunacy.

জুনুনী, A. *adj.* Mad, lunatic.

জুব্বা, A. *n.* A long robe, a cloak.

জুম্লা, A. *n.* Sum, total; a sentence.

জুম্মা, (A. জুময়া). *n.* Friday; the Friday Muhammadan prayers.

জুম্মা-ঘর, A. *n.* A mosque.

জুলমাৎ, A. *n.* Darkness.

জুলাব, (A জুল্লাব). *n.* A purgative.

জুলুম, A. *n.* Injustice, oppression.

জুলুম করা, A. *v.* To oppress.

জুলুমী, A. *adj.* Unjust, oppressive.

জুলুস, A. *n.* A sitting; the accession of a king on the throne.

জুহর, A. *n.* The afternoon just after mid-day; the prayer said at that time.

জুহা, A. *n.* Sacrifice.

জুহুর, A. *n.* Manifestation.

জের, P. *adv.* Beneath, below. *adj.* Inferior; "Brought forward" in book-keeping.

জের টানা, P. *v.* To carry over in an account.

জের করা, P. *v.* To conquer. to subdue.

জেরপাই, P. *n.* Slippers.

জেরবন্দ, P. *n.* A belly-band.

জেরবার, P. *adj.* Overburdened, loaded; exhausted; heavily in debt.

জেরবারী, P. *n.* Expense, debt, liability.

জেরবারী হওয়া, P. *v.* To fall into debt.

জেরা, A. A cross-questioning, a cross-examination.

জেরা করা, A. *v.* To cross-question.

জেরায়ৎ—*See* জিরায়ৎ.

জেলখানা, H. *n.* A prison.

জেলা, A. *n.* A district, a *zillah*; a side; a column on the page of a book.

জেহাদ—*See* জিহাদ.

জৈতুন, A. *n.* An olive.

জৈসা, H. *adv.* As, in like manner. so.

জোৎ, H. *n.* Cultivation. tillage; the holding of a cultivator; the rent paid by a cultivator.

জোৎ জমা, H. *n.* The land cultivated and rent paid by a cultivator.

জোৎদার, H. *n.* A tenure-holder; a farmer.

জোয়ান—*See* জওয়ান.

জোর, A. *n.* Force, strength.

জোরওয়ার, A. *adj.* Strong, powerful.

জোরজবর, A. *n.* Force, violence, oppression.

জোরজবরদস্তী, A. *n.* Tyranny, oppression; violence.

জোরজুলুম, A. *n.* Same as জোরজবর.

জোরু, H. *n.* A wife, a consort.

জোলা, (P. জোলাহা). *n.* A Muhammadan weaver; a fool, a stupid person; a term of abuse.

জোলানী, P. A female *jola.*

জোশ, P. *n.* Emotion; ardour; rage.

জৌজ, A. *n.* A husband.

জৌজা, A. *n.* A wife. (Often written জৌজে.)

জৌজিয়ৎ, A. *n.* The married state.

জৌয়াহির. A. *n.* Jewels.

জৌহর, A. *n.* A jewel, a gem; worth, merit.

জৌহরী, A. *n.* A jeweller,; a dealer in precious stones.

ঝ

ঝকমারী, H. *n.* Foolish talk; a mistake, a lie.

ঝাপ, H. *n.* Wicker-work of bamboo.

ঝাড়া, H. *n.* A stool, excrement.

ঝাড়া ফেরা, H. *v.* To stool, to ease oneself.

ঝাঁড়া লওয়া, H. *v.* To search.

ঝাড়ু, H. *n.* A broom.

ঝিড়কী, H. *n.* Scolding.

ঝীল, H *n.* A lake, a marsh.

ঝুট, H. *n.* A falsehood.

ঝুটা, H. *adj.* False; defiled.

ট

টপ, H. *n.* A leap, a bound.

টপ করিয়া, H. *adv.* Quickly; instantly.

টাট্টী, H. *n.* A privy, a latrine.

টাট্টী যাওয়া, H. *v.* To ease oneself.

টাট্টু, H. *n.* A pony.

টীলা, H. *n.* A low hill, a hillock.

টুকিয়া রাখা. H. *n.* To note down.

টুট, H. *n.* A flaw, a breach.

টুট যাওয়া, H. *v.* To break in pieces; to be shattered.

টোক ফর্দ, P. *n.* A memorandum, a list.

ঠ

ঠাণ্ডা, H. *adj.* Cool, refreshing. *n.* Coldness.

ঠাণ্ডা করা, H. *n.* To cool; to appease.

ঠিকানা, H. *n.* Site, place, abode, address: exact information, trace.

ঠীক, H. *adj.* Accurate, exact; true, right, proper.

ঠীকা, H. *n.* Work done by contract.

ঠীকাদার, H. *n.* A contractor, a lease-holder.

ঠীকুজী. H. *n.* Horoscope.

ড

ডর, H. *n.* Fear.

ডরা, H. *v.* To fear.

ডাকু, H. *n.* A dacoit, a robber.

ডীরা, H. *n.* A tent, a camp.

ডিহি, P. *n.* A district, a village.

ডিহিদার, P. *n.* A district officer, a revenue officer.

ডিহিবন্দী, P. *n.* The assessment of the revenues of a small district.

ত

তওয়কা, A. *n.* Hope, reliance; agreement.

তওয়কুল, A. *n.* Trust, reliance, resignation.

তওয়জ্জহ্, A. *n.* A turning towards, inclination; attention, favour.

তওয়াজা, A. *n.* Humility; attention; a gift, hospitality.

তওয়াজা করা, A. *v.* To entertain; to present a gift.

তওয়াফ, A *n.* Circuit, circumambulation.

তওয়ারীখ, A. *n.* Annals, chronicles, histories. (*Plu.* of তারীখ).

তওলদ হওয়া, A. *v.* To be born.

তক, H. *adv.* Till, until; up to.

তক্ওয়া, A. *n.* Piety, abstinence, chastity.

তক্‌দীর, A. *n.* Fate.

তক্‌ফীন, A. *n.* Burial; shrouding (a dead body).

তক্‌বীর, A. *n.* The expression '*Allahu akbar,*' 'God is Great.'

তকব্বুর, A. *n.* Hauteur, pride.

তক্‌মা, P. *n.* A button, a loop.

তক্‌মিনা, P. *n.* A paper showing details of *khamar* land and its produce.

তক্‌রার, A. *n.* Repetition; dispute, controversy; litigation.

তক্‌রার করা, A. *v.* To quarrel; to argue, to dispute.

তক্‌রারী, A. *adj.* Contentious, disputatious; importunate; disputed.

তক্‌রীর, A. *n.* A speech, a discourse; argument, reasoning.

তক্‌রীরী, A. *adj.* Disputatious, argumentative. *adv.* By word of mouth.

তক্‌লীদ, A. *n.* Imitation, counterfeit, a copy.

তক্‌লীদী, A. *adj.* Imitated, forged, copied.

তক্‌লীফ, A. *n.* Trouble, affliction, difficulty.

তক্‌সীম, A. *n.* Division, partition; a share,

তক্‌সীর, A. *n.* A fault, a crime; an omission, a failure.

তক্‌সীরদার, A. *adj.* Faulty, criminal.

তক্‌সীরমন্দ, A. *adj.* Faulty, criminal.

তক্ত—*See* তখৎ.

তক্তপোস—*See* তখ্‌তাপোশ.

তক্তা, (P. তখ্‌তা) *n.* A plank, a board; a platform.

তক্তানামা, P. *n.* A palanquin.

তকাদা, A. *n.* A claim, a pressing, a dunning; urgency. (Often written তাগাদা.)

তকাদা করা, A. *v.* To hurry, to incite.

তকাবী, (A. তকাওই) *n.* Money lent by Government to farmers at little or no interest.

তকিয়া, P. *n.* A pillow; support, reliance.

তকিয়াদার, P. A Muslim religious mendicant.

তখ্‌ৎ, P. *n.* A throne, a chair.

তখ্‌তাপোশ, P. *n.* A bedstead; a cushion to sit on.

তখ্‌তা, P. *n.* A plank, a board. (Generally written তক্তা.)

তখ্‌তী, P. *n.* A small board, a tile: an amulet on which is written Quranic verses.

তখ্‌ফীফ, A. *n.* A lightening, abatement, remission.

তখ্‌মা, P. *n.* A certificate, a medal.

তগ্‌লব, A. *n.* Cheating, imposition.

তগ্‌লবী, A. *adj.* Counterfeit, adulterated.

তগাইর, A. *n.* Alteration, change; falsification.

তগাবী, *See* তকাবী.

তজকরা, A. *n.* Biography, memoirs.

তজকীয়া, A. *n.* Purification.

তজদীক, A. *n.* Verification, attestation.

তজবীজ, (A. তজওইজ) *n.* Enquiry, examination, search; plan, judgment.

তজম্মুল, A. *n.* Splendour, magnificence.

তজল্লী, A. *n.* Brightness.

তদ্‌বীর, A. *n.* Conduct, management, arrangement.

তদ্‌বীর করা, A. *v.* To manage, to arrange.

তদারক, A. *n.* Investigation; precaution; management, arrangement.

তন্‌, P. *n.* The body.

তন্‌কীহ্‌, A. *n.* Investigation, search.

তন্‌খা—*See* তন্‌খুয়া.

তন্‌খুয়া, P. *n.* Enquiry, search; guess; wages, an order for money, a bill of exchange.

তন্‌খুয়াদার, P. *n.* One who receives wages.

তন্‌খুয়াদারী, P. *n.* The receiving of wages.

তনাকদ, A. *n.* Contradiction.

তনুর, P. *n.* A furnace, an oven. (Sometimes written তন্দুর).

তন্দরস্ত, P. *Adj.* Healthy.

তন্দরস্তী, P. *n.* Health.

তন্দুর, P. *n.* An oven. (*Cor.* of তনুর.)

তপাস, A (?) *n.* Search, investigation.

তফজ্জুল, A. *n.* Kindness, favour.

তফ্‌রীক্‌, A. *n.* Separation, division; a judicial divorce pronounced by a kazi.

তফ্‌সীর, A. *n.* A commentary, an explanation.

তফ্‌সীল, A. *n.* Separation, division, explanation; details, particulars.

তফাৎ, (A. তফাওয়ৎ). *n.* Distance; difference. *adj.* Absent, distant; distinct, separate.

তফাৎ করা, A. *v.* To remove, to place at a distance, to separate.

তফীল, A. *n.* A medium, intervention, mediation. (*See* under তহ্‌বীল.)

তবক, A. *n.* A region ; a kingdom ; a crust, a layer. T. *n.* A gun, a cannon.

তবকা, A. *n.* A storey ; a stage ; a layer ; a shelf ; rank. (Sometimes written তবকত.)

তবকী, T. *n.* One using a gun.

তবকে তবকে, A. *adv.* In layers.

তবতক, H. *adv.* So long as, until.

তবক্কা—*See* তওক্কা.

তব্‌দীল, A. *n.* Change, alteration.

তবন—*See* তহবন্দ.

তবয়ী, A. *adj.* Artificial.

তবল, A. *n.* A drum.

তবলচী, P. *n.* One who plays a drum.

তবাক, A. *n.* A large dish or tray.

তবাজা—*See* তওয়াজা.

তবাহী, P. *n.* Destruction, ruin.

তবীব, A. *n.* A doctor, a physician.

তবীয়ৎ, A. *n.* Health, temperament ; nature.

তবীল—*See* তহবীল.

তমসস্থক, A. *n.* A bond, a note of hand ; a receipt.

তম্‌সীল, A. *n.* An allegory, a parable.

তম্‌হীদ, A. *n.* Preface, introduction.

তমাচা, T. *n.* A slap, a blow.

তমাদী, A. *n.* Duration, time, period ; protraction.

তমাদী হওয়া, A. *v.* To be completed (of a period), to expire.

তমাম, A. *n.* The whole, total. *adj.* Complete.

তমাম করা, A. *v.* To complete, to finish.

তমামী, A. *n.* Completeness.

তমাশা, A. *n.* An exhibition, a spectacle, a sport ; a jest. (Often written তামাসা.)

তমাশা করা, A. *v.* To make fun ; to jest ; to exhibit a spectacle.

তমীজ, A. *n.* Distinction, discrimination.

তমীজ করা, A. *v.* To discriminate.

তম্বী, (A. তম্বীহ) *n.* Punishment ; threat ; persecution.

তয়দাদ, A. *n.* Number, enumeration.

তয়ম্মুম, A. *n.* Ceremonial purification with sand when water is not available.

তয়াল্লুক, A. *n.* Connection, relation.

তয়ালা, A. *adj.* High. Often written তালা as খোদাতালা, the Most High God.

তয়ীন, A. *n.* Settlement, appointment.

তয়ীনাৎ করা, A. *v.* To appoint ; to put in possession.

তর, P. *adj.* Moist, wet ; intoxicated.

তরী, P. *n.* Wetness, moisture ; swamp.

তরওয়াল, H. *n.* A sword.

তরক, A. *n.* Desertion ; relinquishment.

তরক করা, A. *v.* To leave, to forsake ; to give up.

তরকশ, P. *n.* A quiver.

তরক্কী, A. *n.* Progress, improvement, promotion.

তরকারী, P. *n.* Esculent vegetables, a curry ; *tarkari*.

তরজ, A. *n.* Way, form, manner.

তরজা, A. *n.* Antiphonal singing.

তর্জ্জমা, A. *n.* A translation.

তর্জ্জমা করা, A. *v.* To translate.

তর্তীব, A. *n.* Arrangement, order, classification. *adj.* Serial, consecutive.

তর্দুদ, A. *n.* Consideration, deliberation, hesitation ; anxiety.

তরফ, A. *n.* A side, a party ; a portion of village lands. *adv.* On the part of.

তরফদার, A. *n.* A partisan ; the holder of a *taraf*. *adj.* One-sided, partial.

তরফদারী, A. *n.* Partisanship ; partiality.

তরফসানী, A. *n.* A defendant.

তরফে, A. *adv.* On behalf of.

তর্বিয়ৎ, A. *n.* Education, etiquette.

তর্বুজ, P. *n.* A water-melon. (Also written তরমুজ.)

তর্মীম, A. *n.* Amendment, revision, modification ; improvement.

তরমুজ—*See* তর্বুজ.

তরহ, A. *n.* Form, manner, plan ; kind ; like.

তরাজু, P. *n.* Scales, balances.

তরীক, A. *n.* Road ; manner, custom.

তরীকা, A. (Also written তরীকৎ) *n.* Rule, custom, manner.

তলওয়ার, H. *n.* A sword.

তলওয়ারদার, H. *n.* A swordsman.

তলখ, P. *adj.* Bitter.

তলব, A. *n.* Desire, wish, request ; summons ; wages ; an instalment of rent.

তলব করা, A. *v.* To ask ; to summon ; to request.

তলব বাকী, A. *n.* Instalment of rent overdue.

তলবানা, A. *n.* A fee for serving a summons.

তলবানা দাখিল করা, *v.* To pay a witness-fee in court.

তলব চিঠি, A. *n.* A written request.

তলবদস্তক, A. *n.* A summons, a process, a writ.

তলবনামা, A. *n.* A summons, a warrant.

তল্লাশ, (T. তলাশ) *n.* A search, investigation.

থানা-তল্লাশ, A house-search by police officers.

তল্লাশী, T. A seeker, a searcher.

তলাও, P. *n.* A tank, a reservoir. (Also written তলাব.)

তলাক, A. *n.* A divorce, a repudiation. (Generally written তালাক.)

তশত, P. *n.* A large basin.

তশ্‌রীহ, A. *n.* Explanation, exposition.

তশ্‌খীস, A. *n.* Description, specification ; estimate, assessment.

তশ্‌খীস করা, A. *v.* To distinguish, to ascertain.

তশ্‌বীহ, A. *n.* A simile, an allegory.

তশ্‌রীফ, A. *int.* 'Your honour.' Sir ! *n.* Honour, respect.

তস্ওয়ফ, A. *n.* Mysticism ; Sufi theology.

তস্ওয়ীর, A. *n.* A picture, a likeness. (Also written তস্বীর.)

তস্ওয়ীর করা, A. *v.* To imagine.

তসকীন, A. *n.* Satisfaction, comfort. *adj.* Satisfied.

তসদীক, A. *n.* Attestation, verification, confirmation ; an exhibit (in a law court.)

তসদীক করা, A. *v.* To testify, to certify ; to confirm.

তসদীয়া, A. *n.* Trouble, difficulty.

তসনীফ, A. *n.* A composition, an original work.

তসবীর—*See* তসওয়ীর.

তসবীহ, A. *n.* Adoration ; the praise of God by repeating the words *Subhan Allah*; a rosary.

তসমা, P. *n.* A thong, a strap.

তসরুফ, A. *n.* Expenditure ; use ; embezzlement ; holding anything at one's disposal.

তহবীল তসরুফ, A. *n.* Embezzlement of a fund.

তসলা, H. *n.* A brass cooking utensil.

তসলীম, A. *n.* Salutation, greeting ; admission, acknowledgment.

তসলীম করা, A. *v.* To salute ; to admit, to take for granted.

তসল্লী, A. *n.* Consolation, comfort ; assurance, satisfaction.

তহ, P. *n.* Bottom ; surface ; stratum.

তহকীক, A. *n.* Investigation ; certainty ; *adj.* Established, authentic, certain.

তহকীক করা, A. *v.* To ascertain, to investigate ; to make certain.

তহজ্জুদ, A. *n.* A Muslim prayer said after midnight.

তহবন্দ, P. *n.* A cloth worn round the waist.

তহবীল, (A. তহওয়ীল) *n.* Care, trust ; a treasury, a fund, a deposit.

মৌজুদ তহবীল, Cash in hand.

তহবীলদার, A. *n.* A treasurer, a cashier.

তহবীলদারী, A. *n.* The office of a cashier or treasurer.

তহবীল ভাঙ্গা, A. *v.* To embezzle, to defalcate.

তহমৎ, A. *n.* Accusation, suspicion ; calumny.

তহমতী, A, *adj.* Suspicious. *n.* An accuser, a slanderer.

তহরীফ, A. *n.* Alteration, falsification.

তহরীফ করা, A. *v.* To alter, to falsify.

তহরীফ লফজী, A. *n.* Alteration of the text of a document or book.

তহরীফ মানোই, A. *n.* Alteration of the meaning by false exegesis.

তহরীর, A. *n.* A written statement ; a deed, a bond, a fee for writing anything.

তহলীল, A. *n.* Repetition of the Muslim creed.

তহসীল, A. *n.* Acquisition, gain ; the collecting of revenue or rents ; the revenue jurisdiction of a *tahsildar*.

তহসীল করা, A. *v.* To get, to acquire ; to collect revenue or rent.

তহসীলদার, A. *n.* A collector of Government revenue or rent.

তহসীলদারী, A. *n.* The occupation of a *tahsildar*.

তহারৎ, A. *n.* Washing, ablution ; purification.

তাও, (P. তাব) *n.* Heat, anger ; a fold.

তাওয়ীজ, A. *n.* Asking protection of God. (*See* under তা'বীজ)

তাওহীদ,—*See* তৌহীদ.

তাক, A. *n.* An arch, a recess in a wall; a shelf. *adj.* Unequalled, unrivalled.

তাকৎ, A. *n.* Power, strength, ability.

তাকাবী—*See* তকাবী.

তাকিয়া—*See* তকিয়া.

তাকীদ, A. *n.* Confirmation; compulsion; an order, an injunction; a reminder.

তাকীদী, A. *adj.* Emphatic, urgent.

তাখীর, A. *n.* Delay.

তাগাদা—*See* তকাদা.

তাজ, P. *n.* A crown, a diadem.

তাজগী, P. *n.* Freshness, ripeness, newness.

তাজা, P. *adj.* Fresh, green, juicy.

তাজী, A. *n.* An Arabic horse or dog.

তাজীম, A. *n.* Respect.

তাজীয়ৎ, A. *n.* Lamentation, mourning, condolence.

তাজীয়া, A. *n.* A representation of the tombs of Hasan and Husain carried at the *Mohurrum*.

তাজীয়ানা, P. *n.* A whip, a scourge: punishment.

তাজের, A. *n.* A merchant, a trader.

তাজ্জুব, A. *n.* Wonder, surprise.

তাজ্জুব করা, A. *v.* To wonder, to admire.

তানপুরা, (A. তন্‌বুরা). *n.* A stringed musical instrument; a mandoline.

তাপ, (P. তাব), *n.* Heat; anger.

তাফ্‌তাহ, P. *n.* A garment made of a special kind of silk.

তাব, P. *n.* Endurance: power; light.

তাব লওয়া, P. *v.* To endure, to bear.

তাবীজ, A. *n.* An ornament worn on the arm or waist as a charm; an amulet.

তাবুৎ, A. *n.* A coffin. a bier; a representation of the tombs of Hasan and Husain carried in the *Mohurrum* ceremony.

তা'বে, A. *n.* A dependant, a follower; *Esp.* used of those Muslims who knew the personal companions of Muhammad.

তাবেদার, A. *adj.* Subject to, obedient, following, subordinate to.

তাবেদারী, A. *n.* Subjection, obedience; discipleship, allegiance.

তাবেদারী করা, A. *v.* To serve; to follow; to obey.

তামা, (A. তমা) *n.* Greed, avarice.

তামাদী—*See* তমাদী.

তামাশা, (A. তমাশা). *n.* An exhibition, a spectacle; a sport, a jest.

তামাম—*See* তমাম.

তামীল, A. *n.* Performance, operation, execution.

তামীল করা, A. *v.* To put into execution, to perform.

তাম্বু (A. তন্‌বু) *n.* A tent.

তাম্মুল, A. *n.* Hesitation, delay.

তাম্মুল করা, A. *v.* To reflect, to consider; to delay.

তায়দাদ, A. *n.* A deed by which a free grant is made; number, amount.

তায়েদ, A. *n.* Help, aid, support; corroboration.

তায়েদ এজাহার, A. *n.* A corroborative statement.

তায়েদদার, A. *n.* A helper.

তায়েফা, A. *n.* A tribe; a troop, a retinue, a band.

তার, P. *n.* A wire, a thread.

তারীক, A. *adj.* Dark, cloudy; obscure.

তারীকী, A. *n.* Darkness; obscurity.

তারীখ, A. *n.* Date; day of the month; history; era.

তারীখী, A. *adj.* Historical.

তারীফ, A. *n.* Praise; description; *tariff.*

তালা—*See* তয়ালা.

তালাক, (A. তলাক). *n.* A divorce; a repudiation.

তালাকনামা, A. *n.* A bill of divorcement.

তালাক দেওয়া, A. *v.* To divorce.

তালাব, P. *n.* A tank, a cistern, a pond. (Sometimes written তলাও.)

তালিব, A. *n.* A seeker, an enquirer.

তালিব-ইলম, A. *n.* A student.

তালীকা, A. *n.* A list, a catalogue, an inventory.

তালীম, A. *n.* Teaching, instruction.

তালীম দেওয়া, A. *v.* To teach.

তালুক, (A. তয়ল্লুক). *n.* A possession, an estate; a district.

তালুকদার, A. *n.* The holder of a *taluk*; a land-owner.

তালুকদারী, A. *n.* The office or work of a *talukdar.*

তালেবর, A. *adj.* Rich, wealthy; respectable; fortunate.

তাস, A. *n.* Playing cards; brocade.

তাসা, A. *n.* A kettle-drum.

তাহের, A. *adj.* Holy, pure, chaste.

তিজারৎ, A. *n.* Trade, commerce.

তিজারতী, A. *adj.* Pertaining to trade, mercantile.

তিজারতী করা, A. *v.* To trade.

তিফল, A. *n.* A child.

তিফ্লৎ, A. *n.* Childhood.

তিব, A. *n.* Medicine.

তিব্বী, A. *adj.* Medical.

তিলাওয়ৎ, A. *n.* A reading, a recitation.

তীর, P. *n.* An arrow.

তীরান্দাজ, P. *n.* An archer, a bowman.

তীরান্দাজী, P. *n.* Archery.

তুর্কী, P. *n.* Turkey, *adj.* Turkish.

তুহফা, A. *adj.* Rare, excellent. *n* A rarity.

তুফান, A. *n.* A wave; a tempest; a flood.

তুফানী, A. *adj.* Tempestuous.

তুমার, P. *n.* A heap; a list; a register; a personal enquiry into the resources of a *mahal*; an audit.

তুমার জমা, P. *n.* Rent ascertained by personal enquiry.

তেজ, P. *adj.* Sharp, acute, hot, swift, keen. *n.* Heat; sharpness; brilliancy.

তেজারৎ—*See* তিজারৎ.

তেজী, P. *n.* Sharpness, swiftness; heat; brilliancy.

তেরিজ, A. *n.* Addition, amount, total; a zemindari document giving particulars of landed property.

তেসরা, P. *adj.* Third ; the third day of the month.

তৈরমুম—*See* তয়মুম.

তৈয়ার, P. *adj.* Ready, prepared, finished, developed.

তৈয়ার করা, P. *v.* To make to prepare.

তৈয়ারী, P. *n.* Readiness, quickness.

তৈসা, H. *adv.* As (*See* জৈসা).

তোপ, T. *n.* A cannon, artillery.

তোপ দাগা, T. *v.* To fire a cannon.

তোপখানা, T. *n.* An artillery park.

তোপচী, T. *n.* An artilleryman.

তোফা, P. *adj.* Good, beautiful ; rare.

তোশক, P. *n.* A mattress, bedding.

তোশা, P. *n.* Supplies, provisions for a journey ; alms given on the death of a Muslim

তোশাখানা, P. *n.* A storehouse.

তৌক, A. *n.* A collar, a necklace ; fetters, handcuffs.

তৌজী, A. *n.* A rent-roll ; assessment ; an account, a statement.

তৌজীমহল, A. *n.* A *mahal* recorded in a rent-roll.

তৌফীক, A. *n.* Grace, favour ; means. power.

তৌফীর, A. *n.* Increase, excess.

তৌবা, A. *n.* Repentance, penitence.

তৌবা পড়া, A. *v.* To repent. (*Esp.* to publicly embrace Islam.)

তৌরেৎ, A. *n.* The Torah. The books of Moses. The Old Testament.

তৌলীদ, A. *n.* Birth, generation.

তৌহীদ, A. *n.* The worship of the one God. Unity.

থ

থাক, H. *n.* A masonry boundary pillar.

থাকবস্ত, H. *n.* A document showing the boundaries.of land.

থোক, H. *n.* A share ; a tenure ; a total amount.

থোকদার, H. *n.* The holder of a *thok.*

থোকবস্ত, H. *n.* A survey of land in order to fix the boundaries.

থোকা, H. *n.* A written statement of rents due or paid ; a zemindar's rent-roll.

থোড়া, H *adj.* Little, few.

দ

দওয়া—*See* দোয়া.

দওয়ৎ, A. *n.* A feast.

দওয়াৎ—*See* দোয়াৎ.

দঃ Used as an abbreviation for দক্ষিণ.

দখল, A. *n.* The entering into a place, occupancy, taking possession of a place ; the mastery of a subject, proficiency.

দখলী, A. *adj.* Having possession, possessed, as দখলী জমী, land which has been taken possession of ; দখলী স্বত্ব a possessory right, a right of occupancy.

দখল করা, A. *v.* To take possession of, to occupy ; to enter.

দখলকার, A. *n.* A possessor, an occupant.

দখলকারী, A. *n.* Occupancy.

দখল দেহানী, A. *n.* Delivery of possession.

দখলনামা, A. *n.* A document giving right of possession.

দখলে আনা, A. *v.* To enter into possession.

দখলে রাখা, A. *v.* To keep, to retain.

ভোগদখল করা, A. *v.* To enjoy all the rights of possession.

দগা—*See* দেগা.

দঙ্গ, P. *adj.* Astonished, amazed.

দঙ্গা, H. *n.* A riot, a disturbance.

দঙ্গা করা, H. *v.* To riot, to make a disturbance. (Often written দাঙ্গা.)

দজ্জাল, A. *n.* A liar ; an impostor ; anti-Christ. *adj.* Quarrelsome.

দফ্‌তর, A. *n.* A register, a record ; an official report ; a note-book. (Also written দপ্তর.)

দফ্‌তরী, A. *n.* An office-keeper, a record-keeper ; a librarian ; a book-binder.

দফ্‌তরখানা, A. *n.* A record-room ; an office.

দফন, A. *n.* Burial, interment.

দফন করা, A. *v.* To bury.

দফা, A. *n.* One time, once, a moment ; a section, a paragraph ; a page ; a printed form.

দফা করা, A. *v.* To ward off, to repel, to avert.

দফাদফা, A. *adv.* Again and again.

দফাদার, A. *n.* A junior officer of infantry or cavalry ; a subordinate officer placed over village watchmen.

দফাদারী A. *n.* The work of a *dafadar*.

দফারফা, A. *n.* End, conclusion ; ruin.

দফে, A. *adv.* Again, also.

দবদবা, A. *n.* Dignity, state, majesty ; power.

দম, P. *n.* Breath, breathing ; life ; space ; moment.

হরদম, Continually ; every moment.

দম দেওয়া, P. *v.* To wind (a watch).

দমকল, P. *n.* A suction pump.

দমকা, P. *n.* A gust (of wind). *adj.* Sudden, unexpected.

দমদমা, P. *n.* A mound ; a raised emplacement for cannon.

দমবাজ, P. *n.* A cheat, a deceiver.

দমবাজী, P. *n.* Deception, cheating.

দর, P. *n.* A door. *pre.* At, in, on, into ; 'sub' as

দর ইজারা, A sub-lease ; an under-tenure.

দরইয়াফ্‌ৎ, P. *n.* Enquiry, investigation.

দরইয়াফ্‌ৎ করা, P. *v.* To enquire.

দরওয়াজা—*See* দরজা.

দরওয়ান—*See* দরবান.

দরকার, P. *n.* Necessity, want.

দরকারী, P. *adj.* Necessary, needful.

দরখ্‌ৎ, P. *n.* A tree.

দরখাস্ত, P. *n.* A petition, an application ; a request.

দরখাস্ত করা, P. *v.* To make a petition ; to make an application, to proffer a request.

দরখাস্তকারী, P. *n.* A petitioner ; an applicant.

দরগা, (P. দর্‌গাহ) *n.* A Muhammadan shrine ; the tomb of a Muhammadan saint ; a royal court.

দরজা, (P. দরওয়াজা). *n.* A door, a gate.

দরজা, A. *n.* Degree, rank, gradation; dignity.

দরজী, P. *n.* A tailor.

দরদ, P. *n.* Pain; grief; fear.

দরদমন্দ, P. *adj.* Afflicted; compassionate.

বে-দরদ, Unsympathetic, hard-hearted.

দর-দালান, P. *n.* A porch, an outer gateway.

দরদী, P. *adj.* Suffering, afflicted; compassionate.

দর-পত্তনী, P. *n.* A tenure held immediately under a *pattanidar.*

দর-পত্তনী পাট্টা, P. *n.* A lease by which a *pattanidar* transfers his rights to a second person.

দর-পরদার, P. *adv.* Privately, in private. *adj.* Private.

দরপেশ, P. *adv.* In the presence of, before; under trial.

দরপেশ করা, P. *v.* To submit, to lay before.

দরবস্ত,—*See* দরুবস্ত.

দরবান, P. *n.* A porter, a doorkeeper.

দরবার, P. *n.* A hall of audience; a court, a levee,

দরবারীয়া, P. *adj.* Frequenting courts.

দরবেশ, (P. দরওয়েশ). *n.* A religious mendicant; a Muslim devotee, a *dervish.*

দরমা, (P. দরমাহা) *n.* Monthly wages.

দরমাদার, P. *n.* One receiving monthly wages.

দরমিয়ান, P. *adv.* About; in the midst of, between; before.

দরহম,—*See* দিরহম.

দরহম বরহম, P. *adj.* Confounded, jumbled, disorganised; angry.

দরহম বরহম করা, P. *v.* To jumble, to confuse.

দরাজ, P. *adj.* Long, tall; free, open, extensive

দরামদ, P. *n.* Ingress, imports.

দরিয়া, P. *n.* A river; a sea.

দরিয়াফ্‌ৎ—*See* দরইয়াফ্‌ৎ.

দরুণ, P. On account of; reason.

দরূদ, A. *n.* Blessings, praises. *Esp.* a prayer for blessing on Muhammad.

দরূদ পড়া, A. *v.* To pray for blessings on anyone.

দরুবস্ত, P. *adj.* Entire, whole. (Often written দরবস্ত).

দরেন্দা, P. *adj.* Ravenous, ferocious.

দলীজ, (P. দহ্‌লীজ) *n.* A sitting-room; a vestibule, a threshold.

দলীল, A. *n.* Proof, argument; a document.

দলীল দস্তাবেজ, A. *n.* Deeds and documents.

দলীলী, A. *adj.* Containing proofs, as দলীলী কাগজপত্র, papers containing proofs.

দলীলান, A. *adv.* By way of proof.

দলীল পেশ করা, A. *v.* To advance an argument or proof.

দস্ত, P. *n.* A hand; a cubit; a loose stool.

দস্তক, P. *n.* A summons, a judicial writ, a warrant; a fee for serving a summons; a passport; a receipt; a tax.

দস্তখৎ, P. *n.* A signature ; initials ; endorsement.

দস্তখৎ করা, P. *v.* To sign.

দস্তখতী, P. *adj.* Signed ; endorsed.

দস্তবদস্ত, P. *adv.* By hand ; directly, quickly. [withdrawal.

দস্তবরদারী, P. *n.* Relinquishment,

দস্তবরদার হওয়া, P. *v.* To give up, to relinquish.

দস্তরখওয়ান, P. *n.* A table-cloth.

দস্তা, (P. দস্তাহ), *n.* A quire of paper ; a handle.

দস্তানা, P. *n.* A glove.

দস্তাবেজ, (P. দস্তাওয়েজ) *n.* A document, a deed, a bond ; a certificate.

দস্তার, P. *n.* A turban.

দস্তবন্ধক, P. *n.* A pledge.

দস্তী, P. *n.* A present (to a superior) ; a lamp, a torch.

দস্তীদার, P. *n.* One who carries a lamp.

দস্তী সওয়াল, P. *n.* A motion (to a higher court).

দস্তুর, P. *n.* A custom, a habit, a rule ; a regulation.

বে-দস্তুর, contrary to custom.

দস্তুরমত, P. *adv.* According to custom ; completely.

দস্তুরী, P. *n.* Perquisites, commission.

দস্তুর খোদ, P. *adj.* Written with one's own hand.

দহ্লীজ—*See* দলীজ.

দহ্শৎ, A. *n.* Fear.

দহ্শৎজাদা, A. *adj.* Terrified.

দহী, P. *n.* The effigies of Hasan and Husain carried in the Mohurrum ceremony ; the ten days of the Mohurrum during which the *tazias* are carried.

দাই, P. *n.* A midwife ; a wetnurse.

দাওয়ৎ—*See* দওয়ৎ.

দাওয়া, A. *n.* A claim ; an allegation ; a law-suit. (*See* further under দোয়া). [complainant.

দাওয়াদার, A. *n.* A claimant ; a

দাওয়ান—*See* দেওয়ান.

দাওলৎ—*See* দৌলৎ.

দাখিল, A. *n.* The transfer of property ; the delivery of goods ; payment of money.

দাখিল করা, A. *v.* To file (a petition) ; to insert ; to deposit ; to include.

দাখিল হওয়া, A. *v.* To enter ; to be included in ; to occupy.

দাখিলদার, A. *n.* One who transfers something ; a payer.

দাখিল খারেজ, A. *n.* Mutation of names on the occasion of a transfer of property.

দাখিলকারক, A. *n.* A depositor.

দাখিলা, A. *n.* A rent reciept.

দাগ, P. *n.* A mark, a stain, a blot.

দাগ দেওয়া, P. *v.* To mark, to stain, to brand.

দাগবিলি খতিয়ান, P. *n.* A zemindari document showing details of various holdings sub-let to tenants.

দাগা, P. *v.* To mark, to stain, to demarcate ; to fire (a gun or cannon).

দাগী, P. *adj.* Stained, marked. *n.* A man with a bad character.

দাগী চোর, a thief with a previous conviction.

দাঙ্গা, (H. দঙ্গা) *n.* A riot, a disturbance.

দাঙ্গা করা, H. *v.* To make a riot.

দাঙ্গা হাঙ্গামা, H. *n.* A riot, a disturbance.

দাঙ্গাবাজ, H. *adj.* Riotous, quarrelsome.

দাদ, P. *n.* Equity, justice ; revenge ; a gift ; praise.

দাদ তোলা, P. *v.* To take revenge.

দাদ ফরইয়াদ, P. *n.* A prayer for justice.

দাদনী, P. *n.* An advance of money.

দাদনীদার, P. *n.* One who receives an advance of money.

দাদা, H. *n.* A grandfather · father's father.

দাদী, P. *n.* A complainant, a plaintiff ; H. a grandmother, father's mother.

দানা, P. *n.* A seed ; grain. *adj.* Wise.

দানাই, P. *n.* Wisdom, sagacity.

দানেশ, P. *n.* Wisdom.

দানেশমন্দ, P. *adj.* Wise.

দাবী, A. *n.* A claim ; a request ; a complaint.

দাবী করা, A. *v.* To make a claim ; to request.

দাবীদার, A. *n.* A plaintiff ; an accuser ; one who prefers a claim.

দামন, P. *n.* The skirt of a garment ; the foot of a mountain.

দামনগীর, P. *n.* A claimant, a plaintiff, an accuser.

দামাদ, P. *n.* A son-in-law.

দায়ী, A. *n.* A claimant, a plaintiff.

দায়েন, A. *n.* A creditor.

দায়েম, A. *adv.* Always, perpetually.

দায়েমী, A. *adj.* Perpetual, permanent. (As opposed to মিয়াদী, for a period).

দায়ের, A. *adj.* Pending ; in process.

দায়ের করা, A. *v.* To file or institute a suit.

দায়েরা. A. *n.* A circle : a trial.

দায়েরা আদালত, the sessions court.

দায়ূদ, A. *n.* David.

দার, A. *n.* A house, a dwelling ; a monastery.

দার উল্-আখিরৎ, the next world.

দার-উস্-সালাম, the house of peace, heaven.

দার-উল্-আমান, the house of safety, *i.e.* a country where it is unlawful to wage *jehad.*

দার-উল্-হরব, a house of war, *i.e.* a country in which *jehad* is obligatory.

দার, P. A suffix denoting having, holding etc. as জমীনদার, one who holds land, a *zemindar.*

দারোগা, P. *n.* A headman, a police-officer.

জেল-দারোগা, a jailor.

দালান, P. *n.* A masonry building.

দর দালান, the outer hall of a masonry building.

দালাল, A. *n.* A broker, an agent.

দালালী, A. *n.* Brokerage.

দিক, A. *n.* Trouble, vexation, annoyance.

দিক্দার. A. *adj.* Troublesome, vexatious.

দিক্‌দারী, A. *n.* Trouble, vexation.
দিমাগ—*See* দেমাগ.
দিয়ানৎ, A. *n.* Honesty, integrity.
দিয়ানৎদার, A. *adj.* Honest, pious.
দিয়ানৎদারী, A. *n.* Honesty, piety.
দিরহম, A. *n.* A silver coin.
দিল—*See* দেল.
দিস্তা—*See* দস্তা.
দীওয়ান—*See* দেওয়ান.
দীওয়ানা, P. *adj.* Mad.
দীওয়ান্‌গী, P. *n.* Madness.
দীদার, P. *n.* Sight, view.
দীদার্জ, P. *adj.* Conspicuous, handsome.
দীন, A. *n.* Religion, faith.
দীনদার, A. *adj.* Religious, pious.
দীনদারী, A. *n.* Religiousness, piety.
দীনার, A. *n.* Án Arabian gold coin.
দীনী, A. *adj.* Religious, spiritual.
দুতরফা, A. *adj.* Relating to both sides, mutual.
দুন—*See* দোন.
দুনিয়া, P. *n.* The world.
দুনিয়াদার, P. *adj.* Worldly.
দুনিয়াদারী, P. *n.* Worldliness.
দুম্‌, P. *n.* A tail ; an end.
দুমচী, T. *n.* The girth of a saddle.
দুম্বা, (P. দুম্‌বাহ্) *n.* A sheep. *Esp.* a Persian sheep having a thick, heavy tail.
দুয়া—*See* দোয়া.
দুয়েম, P. *adj.* Second, inferior. (Used of a twelve anna crop, or of land which produces a twelve anna crop, as দুয়েম জমী).
দুরমুশ, H. A rammer.
দুরস্ত, P. *adj.* Right, proper, just.
দুল্‌হা, H. *n.* A bridegroom.
দুল্‌হিন, H. *n.* A bride.
দুলিচা, P. *n.* A carpet.
দুশ্‌মন, P. *n.* An enemy.
দুশ্‌মনী, P. *n.* Enmity, hostility.
দুশ্‌মনী করা, P. *v.* To act with enmity ; to oppose.
দূরবীন, P. *n.* A telescope.
দুসরা, P. *adj.* Second. The second day of the month.
দেওয়ান, (P. দীওয়ান) *n.* A minister of state, a steward, a manager, a *diwan ;* a royal court, a court of audience ; a book of poems.
দেওয়ানখানা, P. *n.* A place where a *diwan* transacts his business ; a hall of audience : a court.
দেওয়ানী, P. *adj.* Civil (not criminal). দেওয়ানী আদালৎ, the civil court.
দেওয়াল, (P. দীওয়ার) *n.* A wall.
দেক্‌, (P. দেগ্‌) *n.* A copper vessel, a cauldron.
দেক্‌ছী, (P. দেগ্‌ছী) *n.* A copper vessel, a cauldron, a *dekchi*. (Properly the word refers to a small *dek* only.)
দেগর, P. *adj.* Other, another.
দেগা, A. *n.* Deceit, imposture, fraud.
দেগাদার, A. *adj.* Crafty, deceitful. *n.* A cheat, an impostor.
দেগাবাজ, A. *n.* A cheat, an impostor.
দেগাবাজী, A. *n.* Cheating, imposture.
দেন-মোহর, A. *n.* A dower paid to a Muhammadan bride.
দেনা, (A. দায়েন) *n.* A debt, liability.
দেনাদার. A. *n.* A debtor.
দেনাদারী, A. *n.* Indebtedness.
দেনাপানা, A. *n.* Assets and liabilities.

দেনেওয়ালা, H. *n.* A giver.
দেমাগ, A. *n.* Brain, intellect ; pride, arrogance.
দেমাগী, A. *adj.* Proud, arrogant.
দেমাগদার, A. *adj.* Proud, haughty, insolent.
দেয়ান—*See* দেওয়ান.
দেয়াল—*See* দেওয়াল.
দেরি, P. *n.* Lateness, delay.
দেরি করা, P. *v.* To delay, to be late.
দেল, P. *n.* The heart, the mind.
দেলখুশ, P. *adj.* Pleasing to the heart, enchanting, attractive.
দেলগীর, P. *adj.* Troubled in mind, distressed.
দেলগীরী, P. *n.* Sorrow, distress.
দেলদার, P. *n.* A lover, a mistress.
দেলাবর, (P. দেলাওয়র). *adj.* Brave, intrepid.
দেলাসা, P. *n.* Comfort, consolation.
দেলাসা দেওয়া, P. *v.* To comfort, to console ; to encourage.
দেলীর, P. *adj.* Daring, intrepid.
দেশমশহুর, A. *adj.* Known or famous throughout a country.
দো, H. *adj.* Two. (Used much in compounds, as দো-পায়া, having two legs.)
দোকর, H. *n.* Repetition. *adv.* Again.
দোকান, P. *n.* A shop.
দোকান করা, P. *v.* To keep a shop.
দোকানদার, P. *n.* A shop-keeper.
দোকানদারী, P. *n.* Shop-keeping.
দোকানদারী করা, P. *v.* To pursue the vocation of a shop-keeper.
দোকানী, P. *n.* A retail shop-keeper.
দোখ্‌তর, P. *n.* A daughter.
দোজখ, P. *n.* Hell.
দোজখী, P. *adj.* Hellish, infernal. *n.* An inhabitant of hell.
দোন, H. *adj.* Both.
দোয়া, A. *n.* A prayer, supplication ; a blessing. (Extempore and voluntary prayer as distinguished from the ritual *salat.*)
দোয়া করা, A. *v.* To bless. [pray.
দোয়া মাঙ্গা, A. *v.* To supplicate, to
দোয়াৎ, A. *n.* An inkstand.
দোরেম—*See* দুরেম.
দোরস্ত—*See* দুরস্ত.
দোসরা—*See* দুসরা.
দোস্ত, P. *n.* A friend, a companion.
দোস্তদার, P. *adj.* Friendly.
দোস্তদারী, P. *n.* Friendship.
দোস্তী, P. *n.* Friendship.
দেওয়া, A. *n.* Medicine ; a cure.
দোয়াখানা, A. *n.* A hospital.
দৌল, P. *n.* State, condition ; estimate ; statement.
দৌলৎ, A. *n.* Wealth, opulence.
দৌলৎমন্দ, A. *adj.* Wealthy, opulent.
দৌলৎদার, A. *adj.* Wealthy, opulent.
দৌলৎখানা, A. *n.* A treasury.

ধ

ধূপ, H. *n.* The sun ; sunshine.
ধোকা, H. *n.* Deception, delusion.
ধোকাবাজ, H. *adj.* Deceitful.
ধোকাবাজী, H. *n.* Deceit.

ন

নওবৎ, A. *n.* Time, turn ; state ; the beating of drums at a rich man's house.
নওবৎখানা, A. *n.* A band-stand, a music-room.

নওয়াজ, P. *n.* A cherisher.

নওয়াজিশ, P. *n.* Kindness, favour, patronage.

নওয়াজিশ করা, P. *v.* To favour, to [patronise.

নওয়াব--*See* নবাব.

নওয়ারা, P. *n.* A large boat, a barge.

নকল, A. *n.* A copy ; imitation ; a transfer, removal.

নকল করা, A. *v.* To copy, to transcribe.

নকলনবীস, A. *n.* A copyist, a clerk.

নকলনবীসী, A. *n.* The act of copying ; the employment of a copyist.

নকলবরদার, A. *n.* A copyist.

নকলবরদারী, A. *n.* The employment of a copyist.

নকস, A. *n.* Defect ; decrease.

নকসান—*See* নোকসান.

নক্‌শা, A. *n.* A map, a plan, a pattern, a portrait.

নক্‌শা করা, A. *v.* To draw (a plan).

নক্‌শাবন্দী, A. *n.* A mendicant sect of Muslims.

নকাশী, A. *n.* A carver, an engraver.

নকীব, A. *n.* A servant ; a herald ; an agent.

নকীর, A. *n.* The name of one of the two angels who are supposed to examine the dead in the tomb.

নক্কাশ, A. *n.* A sculptor, an engraver ; a draughtsman.

নগদ, (A. নকদ). *n.* Cash, ready money.

নগদ কারবার, A. *n.* A cash transaction.

নগদান, A. *n.* A petty cash-book.

নগদী, A. *n.* A bearer of cash or revenue. *adj.* Relating to cash, cash.

নঙ্গর—*See* লঙ্গর.

নঙ্গা, H. *adj.* Naked, bare.

নছীব—*See* নসীব.

নজদীক, P. *adj.* Near, in one's view.

নজদীকী, P. *n.* Nearness, proximity.

নজদীক হওয়া, P. *v.* To draw near, to approach.

নজম, A. *n.* A star.

নজর, A. *n.* A look ; sight ; supervision ; a present to a superior ; an offering ; a vow.

নজর করা, A. *v.* To look, to glance.

নজর রাখা, A. *v.* To watch, to keep in view.

নজর দেওয়া, A. *v.* To make an offering, to present ; to sacrifice.

নজর মানা, A. *v.* To make a vow.

নজরবন্দ, A. *adj.* Guarded, confined ; under surveillance.

নজরবন্দী, A. *n.* Surveillance ; confinement.

নজরবাজ, A. *n.* A juggler.

নজরবাজী, A. *n.* Jugglery.

নজরানা, A. *n.* A present to a superior.

নজাৎ, A. *n.* Salvation, deliverance.

নজাৎ-দেহেন্দা, A. *n.* A saviour.

নজাৎ-দেনেওয়ালা, A. *n.* A saviour.

নজারৎ, A. *n.* The office of a *nazir.*

নজাসৎ, A. *n.* Filth, impurity.

নজীব, A. *adj.* Noble, of noble birth.

নজীর, A. *n.* A precedent : example ; likeness ; quotation.

নজীর দেখান, A. *v.* To refer to a legal precedent.

নজুম, A. *n.* Astrology.

নজুমী, A. *n.* An astrologer.

নজুল—*See* নুজুল.

নতীজা, A. *n.* End; effect, result, consequence; reward.

নথী, H. *n.* The records or papers in a case, a file.

নদামৎ, A. *n.* Shame.

নদারৎ, P. *n.* Lack, want.

নফর, P. *n.* One person; a servant.

নফরী, P. *n.* Daily service or wages.

নফরৎ, A. *n.* Disgust, loathing.

নফল, A. *adj.* Supererogatory, voluntary.

নফ্স্, A. *n.* The soul, the mind, the breath; self; essence; lust.

নফ্সানী, A. *adj.* Sensual, carnal.

নফ্সানীয়ৎ, A. *n.* Sensuality; egotism.

নফা, A. *n.* Profit, gain.

নফাস, A. *n.* The afterbirth; the forty days after childbirth.

নফী, A. *n.* Negation, denial.

নফীরী, P. *n.* A trumpet, a clarionet.

নবাব, (A. নওয়াব) *n.* A governor; a Muslim nobleman, a *Nawab.*

নবাবী, A. *n.* The office of a *Nawab*; the behaviour of a *Nawab.* (So used of a man who puts on airs).

নবী, A. *n.* A prophet; one inspired. (See under রসূল for difference between the two words.)

নবীরা, P. *n.* A grandson; a son's son.

নবীরী, P. *n.* A grand-daughter; a son's daughter.

নবীস, (P. নওয়ীস) *n.* A writer, a copyist; a secretary.

নবীসী, P. *n.* Writership.

নবূৎ, A. *n.* Propheey.

নমাজ, P. *n.* Muhammadan ritual prayer.

নমাজ পড়া, P. *v.* To pray (the legal prayers).

নমাজী, P. *adj.* Prayerful, devout. *n.* One who says his *namaz.*

নমূদ, P. *n.* Appearance; a spectacle, an outward show; an index.

নমূদ করা, P. *v.* To show, to display.

নমূদার, P. *adj.* Visible, conspicuous.

নমূনা, P. *n.* A pattern, example, model.

নয়ৎ, A. *n.* Description; praise. (Sometimes written নাত).

নয়া, H. *adj.* New, recent.

নরম, P. *adj.* Soft; gentle; mild; dull; defective.

নস, A. *n.* A manifesting; a clear dictum of law which cannot be set aside.

নসখ, A. *n.* The Arabic character (script).

নসখা, A. *n.* A copy; an edition; a prescription.

নসব, A. *n.* Lineage, dynasty.

নসবনামা, A. *n.* A genealogical table.

নসর, A. *n.* Victory, help.

নসল, A. *n.* Lineage, dynasty.

নসারা, A. *n.* A Christian.

নসরাণী, A. *n.* A Christian.

নসীব, A. *n.* Fate, lot, destiny.

নসীহৎ, A. *n.* Advice, counsel admonition.

নশ্তর, P. *n.* A lancet.

নহর, A. *n.* A river, a stream.

না, P. A negative prefix, meaning no, not, as নাপাক impure etc.

নাও, H. *adj.* New, fresh.

নাওকর—*See* নোকর.

নাওবৎ—*See* নওবৎ.

নাওয়া, H. *v.* To bathe. *n.* A bath, an ablution.

নাওয়াজিব, A. *adj.* Unnecessary, improper.

নাওয়াকিফ, A. *adj.* Ignorant, unacquainted with.

নাকিস, A. *adj.* Defective, deficient.

নাকিস করা, A. *v.* To invalidate, to annul ; to render defective.

নাকারা, P. *adj.* Useless, unprofitable ; incompetent.

নাখুন, P. *n.* Talons, claws, nails.

নাখুশ, P. *adj.* Displeased.

নাখেরাজ—*See* লাখ্‌রাজ.

নাখোদা, P. *n.* The captain of a snip.

নাগাইদ—*See* লাগায়েৎ.

নাচার, P. *adj.* Without a remedy, helpless.

নাচারী, P. *n.* Helplessness, hopelessness.

নাজাৎ—*See* নজাৎ.

নাজায়েজ, A. *adj.* Illegal, unlawful.

নাজারী, A. *adj.* Inoperative, not in force.

নাজিম, A. *n.* A governor, an administrator.

নাজীর, A. *n.* A superintendent of peons in a law court ; a superintendent ; a jailor ; an inspector ; a bailiff, a *nazir.*

নাজীরী, H. *n.* The employment of a *nazir.*

নাজীরখানা, A. *n.* The office of a *nazir.*

নাজেরা, A. *n.* The reading of a book. (*Esp.* of the Quran).

নাজেল, A. *n.* Alighting, descent.

নাজেল হওয়া, A. *v.* To descend, to come down.

নাজেহাল, P. *adj.* Wretched, miserable.

নাতাব, P. *adj.* Weak, infirm, impotent.

নাতোয়ান, P. *adj.* Weak, infirm.

নাদান, P. *adj.* Ignorant, illiterate ; foolish.

নাদানী, P. *n.* Foolishness, ignorance.

নাদার, P. *adj.* Having nothing, indigent.

নানকর জমী, A. *n.* Maintenance land.

নানা, H. *n.* Maternal grandfather.

নানী, H. *n.* Maternal grandmother.

নাপসন্দ, P. *adj.* Unwelcome, nonpleasing, unacceptable.

নাপাক, P. *adj.* Unclean, impure.

নাপাকী, P. *n.* Impurity.

নাফ, P. *n.* The navel.

নাফরমান, P. *adj.* Disobedient.

নাফরমানী, P. *n.* Disobedience.

নাবালগ, P. *n.* A minor. *adj.* Under age.

নামজাদা, P. *adj.* Famous, well known.

নামঞ্জুর, P. *adj.* Refused, rejected.

নামঞ্জুর করা, P. *v.* To reject, to refuse.

নামদার, P. *adj.* Famous, renowned.

নামা, P. A suffix denoting any written document or deed, as তালাকনামা, a deed of divorce.

নামাজ—*See* নমাজ.

নায়েব, A. *n.* A deputy, a delegate; an agent; a rent-collector, a zemindari officer.

নায়েব নাজিম, A. *n.* Deputy governor, a title formerly applied to certain nawabs of Bengal.

নায়েবী, P. *adj.* Deputyship, agency, the occupation of a *naib*.

নারঙ্গী, P. *n.* An orange.

নারাজ, A. *adj.* Displeased, dissatisfied; unwilling.

নারাজী, A. *n.* Displeasure, dissatisfaction; unwillingness.

নারাস্ত, P. *adj.* Dishonest, faithless.

নারাস্তী, P. *n.* Dishonesty, faithlessness.

নাল, A. *n.* A horse-shoe.

নালবন্দ, A. *n.* A farrier.

নালায়েক, A. *adj.* Unfit, unworthy, improper.

নালিশ, P. *n.* A complaint; a lawsuit a legal action.

নালিশ করা, P. *v.* To complain; to institute a suit.

নালিশী, P. *n.* A complainant, a plaintiff. *adj.* নালিশী সম্পত্তি property in suit.

নাশ্তা, P. *n.* Breakfast.

নাসেখ, A. *n.* A repealing; an injunction (of the Quran) which repeals or invalidates some other injunction. (*See* মনসুখ.)

নাসের, A. *n.* A helper; a defender.

নাস্তানাবুদ, P. *n.* Annihilation. *adj.* Destroyed, ruined.

নাহক, A. *adj.* Unjust; untrue; unrighteous.

নিকলা, H. *v.* To emerge from, to issue.

নিকলিয়া যাওয়া, H. *v.* To emerge from, to issue out of.

নিকলান, H. *v.* To put out, to eject.

নিকা, (A. নিকাহ). *n.* A marriage. (In Bengal the word is generally used amongst Muslims to signify a second marriage.)

নিকা করা, A. *v.* To marry, to wed.

নিকানামা, A. *n.* A marriage contract.

নিকারী, *n.* A Muhammadan fish-merchant.

নিজাম, A. *n.* A governor, administrator; ruler. A title of the rulers of Hyderabad.

নিজামৎ, A. *n.* Administration, organization, arrangement; system. The office of a revenue collector; a criminal court.

নিদা, A. *n.* Call, proclamation.

নিদান, H. *adv.* At length.

নিন্দ, H. *n.* Sleep.

নিয়াজ, A. *n.* Supplication; an offering.

নিয়াজ দেওয়া, A. *v.* To dedicate, to devote.

নিয়াজমন্দ, A. *adj.* Obedient.

নিমক, P. *n.* Salt.

নিমক হারাম, Faithless; ungrateful.

নিমক হালাল, True, faithful.

নিয়ৎ, A. *n.* Intention, design. *Esp.* used of the intention to perform the Muhammadan ritual prayers.

নিয়ামৎ, A. *n.* Grace, favour, bounty.

নিরালা, H. *adj.* Alone, lonely; odd, singular.

নিরিখ, P. *n.* Rate, assessment, price ; the market rate.

নিরিখ করা, P. *v.* To assess ; to mark.

নিরিখবন্দী, P. *n.* A table of rates, a tariff.

নিশা—*See* নেশা.

নিশান, P. *n.* A flag ; a mark ; a signal.

নিশানদিহী, P. *n.* Identification.

নিশানা, P. *n.* Aim, mark.

নিশানী, P. *n.* A sign ; a miracle.

নিশানবরদার, P. *n.* A standard-bearer.

নিশানবরদারী, P. *n.* The office of a standard-bearer.

নিসফ, A. *adj.* Half.

নিসবৎ, A. *n.* Affinity, relationship, connection.

নিসবৎ করা, A. *v.* To ascribe, to attribute, to refer to.

নুজুল, A. *n.* Crown lands ; descent. (*Esp.* of the Quran from heaven.)

নুসখা, A. *n.* A copy.

নুসরৎ, A. *n.* Aid, victory.

নূর, A. *n.* Light ; splendour.

নুরানী, A. *adj.* Bright. *n.* Brightness.

নেওয়াজ, P. *n.* A cherisher.

নেওয়াজী, P. *n.* Kindness, favour.

নেংটা, H. *adj.* Naked.

নেক, P. *adj.* Pure, good, holy, virtuous.

নেকী, P. *n.* Virtue, goodness, righteousness.

নেকনজর, P. *adj.* Having clear sight.

নেকনাম, P. *adj.* Respected, worthy.

নেকবখৎ, P. *adj.* Fortunate, blessed.

নেগা, (P. নেগাহ). *n.* A look, a glance ; attention.

নেগা করা, P. *v.* To view, to inspect.

নেগাদার, P. *n.* A watchman, a guard, a protector.

নেগাদারী, P. *n.* The office of a watchman.

নেগাবান, P. *n.* A watchman, a guard, a protector.

নেগাবানী, P. *n.* The office of a watchman.

নেগাবানী করা, P. *v.* To look after, to watch.

নেজা, P. *n.* A spear, a lance.

নেজাবরদার, P. *n.* A lancer.

নেজামৎ—*See* নিজামৎ.

নেদামৎ—*See* নদামৎ.

নেফা, P. *n.* A seam.

নেবাজ—*See* নেওয়াজ.

নেয়ামৎ—*See* নিয়ামৎ.

নেশা, P. *n.* Intoxication ; an intoxicating liquor ; pride.

নেশা হওয়া, P. *v.* To be intoxicated.

নেশাখোর, P. *n.* A drunkard.

নেশাখোরী, P. *n.* Drunkenness ; fondness for intoxicants.

নেশাবাজ, P. *n.* A drunkard.

নেশাবাজী, P. *n.* Drunkenness.

নেসা, A. *n.* A woman.

নেহাৎ, (A. নেহায়েৎ) *adv.* Very much, extremely.

নেহাল, P. *adj.* Rich, prosperous, fruitful ; pleased.

নোক্তা, A. *n.* A dot, a diacritical mark in Arabic letter-press.

নোকসান, A. *n.* Loss, damage, injury. (Often written লোকসান).

নোকসান জমী, land left without an occupier.

নোকসান জরীপ, land resurveyed after the death or flight of previous occupier.

নোকসানী, A. *adj.* Injurious, detrimental.

নো, P. *adj.* New, young.

নৌকর, P. *n.* A servant, a retainer.

নৌকরী, P. *n.* Service, employment.

নোকরী করা, P. *v.* To serve.

নৌবৎ, A. *n.* Turn, time, succession ; state ; a band of musical instruments.

নৌবৎখানা, A. *n.* A band-stand.

প

পস্ত—*See* পোশ্ তা.

পক্কা, H. *adj.* Ripe, mature, strong, sound, real, certain ; masonry.

পক্কা করা, H. *v.* To strengthen ; to confirm, to settle ; to certify.

পছন্দ—*See* পসন্দ.

পড়োসী, H. *n.* A neighbour.

পঠান, H. *n.* A race of Muslims on the N. W. Indian frontier ; *Pathan*. One of the four classes into which Indian Muslims are divided. (Often written পাঠান.)

পনা, P. *n.* Width.

পনাহ্, P. *n.* A refuge, a shelter.

পনীর, P. *n.* Cheese.

পয়কাস্ত—*See* পাইকশ্ তা.

পয়গাম, P. *n.* An embassage ; an errand, a message.

পয়গম্বর, P *n.* A messenger, a prophet.

পয়গম্বরী, P. *n.* The mission of a prophet.

পয়জার, P. *n.* A slipper, a shoe.

পয়দল, P. *n.* A foot-soldier.

পয়দা, P. *adj.* Born, produced ; manifest, visible.

পয়দা করা, P. *v.* To create.

পয়দায়েশ, P. *n.* Creation, birth.

পয়দায়েশী, P. *adj.* Innate, inborn.

পয়মায়েশ, P. *n.* Measurement.

পয়মায়েশী জমী, P. *n.* Land acquired as the result of a re-measurement.

পয়মাল,—*See* পায়মাল.

পয়রব—*See* পায়রব.

পয়স্তী, P. *n.* (Land) reclaimed from the river for cultivation.

পর, P. *n.* A feather ; a wing ; strength.

পরকলা, P. *n.* Glass ; a looking-glass.

পরওয়া, P. *n.* Need, care, anxiety, fear.

পরওয়ানা, P. *n.* A written order, a command ; a permission ; a patent, a pass, a warrant ; an order of appointment.

পরওয়ানগী, P. *n.* Permission, license.

পরওয়ার, P. *n.* A protector, a preserver ; a patron.

পরওয়ারদেগার, P. *n.* Providence ; God.

পরওয়ারিশ, P. *n.* Protection, support, bringing up.

পরখ, H. *n.* Temptation : examination.

পরখ করা, H. *v.* To tempt ; to examine.

পরগণা, P. *n.* A district ; a fiscal division.

পরচা, P. *n.* Papers and documents ; a slip of paper ; a fragment ; a written description of land, its extent, rent etc.

পরৎ, H. *n.* A layer, a crust.

পরতল জরীপ, A. *n.* A re-survey.

পরব, (H. for পর্ব্ব). *n.* A festival, a feast.

পরীশান, P. *adj.* Distracted, perplexed ; scattered.

পরীশানী, P. *n.* Perplexity, bewilderment ; trouble.

পরীশান করা, P. *v.* To perplex, to harass.

পরস্ত, P. *n.* A suffix signifying a worshipper as বুৎপরস্ত, an idolator.

পরস্তী, P. *n.* Worship.

পরস্তিশ, P. *n.* Worship.

পরহীজ, P. *n.* Abstinence, temperance.

পরহীজ করা. P. *v.* To abstain from.

পরহীজগার, P. *adj.* Abstinent, temperate.

পরহীজগারী, P. *n.* Abstinence.

পরাগন্দা. P. *adj.* Scattered.

পরেন্দা, P. *n.* A bird.

পর্দ্দা, P. *n.* A curtain, a screen, a veil.

পর্দ্দানশীন, P. *n.* One who remains behind a curtain : one who keeps in the *zenana.*

পর্দ্দাপোশ, P. *n.* Concealment of a fault.

পর্দ্দাপোশী, P. *n.* Faithfulness, fidelity.

পলাও, P. *n.*, Rice boiled with meat and spices ; *palao.*

পলীতা, P. *n.* A wick. (From A. ফতীল.)

পশম, P. *n.* Wool, fur.

পশমী, P. *adj.* Woollen.

পশীমান. P. *adj.* Penitent ; ashamed.

পশীমানী, P. *n.* Penitence ; shame.

পসন্দ, P. *n.* Choice, selection ; approval.

পসন্দ করা, P. *v.* To choose ; to approve.

পসলী, H. Ribs. breast.

পস্তান, H. *v.* To repent, to regret.

পহিলা, H. *adv.* First ; before, previously. *n.* The first day of the month.

পাজা, P. *n.* A brick-kiln.

পাইক, P. *n.* A messenger ; a village watchman ; a subordinate officer in a *zemindari.*

পাইকশ্‌তা, P. *n.* Non-resident ;

পাইকশ্‌তা প্রজা, A tenant who cultivates in one place, and lives in another.

পাইকশ্‌তা জমী, land let to or cultivated by a non-resident tenant. (c. f. খোদকশ্‌তা).

পাইকার, P. *n.* A retail dealer who purchases wholesale ; a pedlar.

পাইকারী. P. *adj.* Wholesale.

পাইজামা—*See* পায়জামা.

পাইদার, P. *adj.* Durable, lasting.

পাইমাল—*See* পায়মাল.

পাইরু, P. *n.* A follower, an attendant ; votary of a religious sect.

পাইরুই, P. *n.* Adherence, observance ; investigation ; endeavour.

পাইরুই করা, P. *v.* To follow, to observe ; to adhere to ; to maintain.

পাক, P. *adj.* Pure, clean, holy, unadulterated.

পাক সাফ, P. *adj.* Pure and clean.

পাকী, P. *n.* Purity, cleanliness.

পাকীজগী, P. *n.* Purity, cleanliness.

পাকীজা, P. *adj.* Pure, holy, clean.

পাকড়া, H. *n.* The act of seizing.

পাকড়াও করা, H. *v.* To seize, to capture.

পাকড়ান, H. *v.* To seize, to capture.

পাড়াপরসী, H. *n.* Neighbours.

পাজী, P. *adj.* Low, mean, vulgar; mad. *n.* a rogue, a rascal.

পাজীয়ানা, P. *n.* Lowness, vulgarity; rascality.

পাঞ্জা, P. *n.* The hand; a grasp; five.

পাঞ্জাবী, P. *n.* A boy's garment.

পাট্টা, H. *n.* A deed or lease granted by a zemindar to his tenants.

পাট্টা সেলামী, a cash payment made to a zemindar by his tenant when accepting a lease of land.

পাট্টাদার, H. *n.* One who accepts a lease from a zemindar.

পাটোয়ারী, H. *n.* A keeper of zemindari accounts.

পাঠান—*See* পঠান.

পানী, H. *n.* Rain; water.

পাপোশ, P. *n.* A shoe, a slipper.

পায়খানা, P. *n.* A privy.

পায়জামা, P. *n.* A night-suit; a pair of drawers.

পায়মাল, P *n.* Ruin, devastation. *adj.* Trampled under foot, devastated.

পায়া, P. *n.* A leg; a foot; a support; rank.

পায়ীক—*See* পাইক.

পায়র—*See* পাইর.

পায়রবী—*See* পাইরবী.

পারা, P. *n.* A part, a portion. *Esp.* a thirtieth part of the Quran.

পাল্লা, P. *n.* A scales, a balance.

পালোয়ান, P. *n.* A strong man; a champion. *adj.* Strong.

পাস, H. *adj.* Near, beside; in possession of.

পাহারা, P. *n.* A watchman, a guard.

পাহারা ওয়ালা—*Same as* পাহারা

পাহারা দেওয়া, P. *v.* To keep guard, to watch.

পাহারাদার, P. *n.* One who keeps guard, a watchman.

পিছলী, H. *adj.* Back, rear, last; modern. (Also written পিছলা).

পিনা, H. *v.* To drink.

পিয়ন, P. *n.* A messenger, an orderly, a *peon*, a bailiff of a judicial court.

পিয়াজ, P. *n.* An onion.

পিয়াদা—*See* পেয়াদা.

পিয়ার, H. *n.* Love, affection; friendship.

পিয়ার করা, H. *v.* To love.

পিয়ারা, H. *adj.* Beloved.

পিয়ালা, P. *n.* A drinking-vessel, a cup.

পিয়ালাবাজ, P. *n.* A drunkard.

পিয়ালাবাজী, P. *n.* Drunkenness.

পিয়াস, H. *n.* Thirst; desire, longing.

পিয়াসা, H. *adj.* Thirsty, longing, wishful.

পিরাণ, P. *n.* A long robe; a shirt.

পিলান, H. *v.* To cause to drink.

পীড়হী, H. *n.* A small stool.

পীর, P. *n.* A holy man, a saint; a spiritual guide; the head of a Muhammadan religious order.

পীরাণ, P. *n.* Land given for the support of a *pir*.

পীরোজা, P. *n.* A gem. a turquois.

পীরোত্তর, P. *n.* Rent-free land dedicated to some saint.

পীলপা, (P. পীলপায়া) *n.* A pillar; a prop.

পীলসুজ, (A. ফতীল) *n.* A brass candle-stick or lamp-stand.

পুকার, H. *n.* A cry, a summons, a prayer; a complaint.

পুকারনা, H. *v.* To cry out, to call.

পুদীনা—*See* পোদীনা.

পুল, P. *n.* A bridge

পুলসিরাৎ, a bridge said to be stretched over hell, across which believers will pass in safety on the day of judgment.

পুলবন্দী, P. *n.* An embankment; a tax formerly imposed for the repair of bridges.

পুশীদা—*See* পোশীদা.

পেঁচ, P. *n.* A twist, a winding; perplexity, trouble; the thread of a bolt or screw.

পেঁচ দেওয়া, P. *v.* To screw, to twist.

পেঁচাও, P. *adj.* Winding, twisting, intricate.

পেঁচে ফেলা, P. *v.* To throw into difficulty.

পেঁচানিয়া, P. *adj.* Perplexing, confusing.

পেয়াদা, P. *n.* A foot-messenger; the baliff of a judicial court; a *peon*.

পেয়াদাগিরী, P. *n.* The occupation of a *peada*.

পেয়ার—*See* পিয়ার.

পেরেশান—*See* পরীশান.

পেরোজ—*See* ফেরোজ.

পেলা, H. *n.* A prop.

পেশ, P. *adj.* The front, the forepart, In Persian grammar the vowel u.

পেশ করা, P. *v.* To lay before, to submit, to bring forward.

পেশওয়া, P. *n.* A leader, a guide.

পেশওয়াহী, P. *n.* Leadership, guidance.

পেশওয়াহী করা P. *v.* To guide, to escort.

পেশওয়াজ, P. *n.* A special dress of a female dancer. (Also written পেশবাজ.)

পেশকবজ, P. *n.* A dagger.

পেশকশ, P. *n.* A tax, tribute.

পেশকার P. *n.* A deputy, an agent, an assistant; a court officer next in rank to a *seristadar*; a zemindari officer who has charge of the accounts and documents.

পেশকারী, P. *n.* Deputyship, the office of a *peshkar*.

পেশখবর, P. *n.* Prophecy.

পেশগী, P. *n.* Advance money; a deposit.

পেশগুয়ী, P. *n.* Prophecy.

পেশদার, P. *n.* Trading, trafficking.

পেশদারী, P. *n.* Trade, traffic.

পেশা, P. *n.* A trade, profession; custom.

পেশাকার, P. *n.* A prostitute, a whore.

পেশাদার, P. *n.* A merchant, a trader.

পেশাদারী, P. *n.* Trading, trafficking.

পেশানী, P. *n.* The forehead, the brow ; fate, destiny.

পেশাব, P. *n.* Urine.

পেশীমান—*See* পশীমান.

পেসর, P. *n.* A son, a boy. (Sometimes written পেস্র).

পোক্তা, (P. পোখ্তা) *adj.* Ripe, mature ; complete ; strong.

পোক্তানী, *n.* Ripeness, maturity.

পোচা, H. *n.* The wrist.

পোতা, H. A grandson.

পোদ্দার, P. *n.* A banker ; a money-changer.

পোদ্দারী, P. *n.* A banking business.

পোদীনা P. *n.* Mint.

পোলাও—*See* পলাও

পোলাৎ, *n.* Steel.

পোস্ত, P. *n.* A crust, shell, skin ; a poppy head.

পোস্তা, P. *n.* A buttress, an embankment, a prop.

পোশ, P. A suffix meaning a covering.

চাপোশ, a tea cosy.

সরপোশ, a cover of a *dekchhi.*

বালাপোশ, a quilt : a cover for the head.

পোশীদা, P. *adj.* Hidden, concealed ; secret.

পোশীদা করা, P. *v.* To hide, to conceal.

পৌলী, H. *n.* A door, a threshold.

পৌশাক, P. *n.* Dress, clothing.

পৌশাকী, P. *adj.* Pertaining to clothing.

ফ

ফইজৎ—*See* ফজীহৎ.

ফওয়ারা, P. *n.* A fountain, a spring.

ফকৎ, A. *adj.* Only, simply, solely. *adj.* Alone. *n.* The end.

ফকৎখালী, A.—A word often written at the end of documents to signify completion. Sometimes the word is simply written ফকৎ.

ফকর, A. *n.* Poverty.

ফকীর, A. *adj.* Poor, needy. *n.* A beggar ; the name of a Muslim Sufistic sect in Bengal.

ফকীরানা, A. *n.* Lands appropriated to the support of *fakirs.*

ফকীরী, A. *n.* Poverty ; mendicancy ; the practice of the tenets of the *Fakir* sect.

ফক্কর, (A. ফিক্রা). *n.* A wag ; a cheat.

ফক্করী, A. *n.* Drollery, witticism : deception.

ফক্করবাজ, A. *adj.* Artful, deceitful.

ফক্করবাজী, A. *n.* Deception.

ফখর, A. *n.* Pride ; boast, glory.

ফজর, A. *n.* The dawn, early morning ; the name given to the first of the five Muslim liturgical prayers.

ফজল, A. *n.* Bounty, grace, favour.

ফজীহ, A. *adj.* Disgraceful, vile.

ফজীহৎ, A. *n.* Disgrace, shame ; reproach, infamy : quarrel.

ফটক, H. *n.* A gate : a lock-up.

ফটকবন্দী, H. *n.* Imprisonment, custody.

ফড়িয়া, H. *n.* A pedlar, a retail shop-keeper.

ফৎওয়া, A. *n.* A legal verdict based on Muhammadan ecclesiastical law.

ফৎওয়া দেওয়া, A. *v.* To give a legal decision based on Muhammadan ecclesiastical law.

ফতহ, A. *n.* A victory ; success. (Often written ফতে).

ফতহ করা, A. *v.* To conquer.

ফতহমন্দ, A. *adj.* Victorious.

ফতুর, A. *adj.* Weak, poor. *n.* A defect, unsoundness.

ফন, A. *n.* Art, accomplishment.

ফনা, A. *adj.* Passed away, departed, non-existent.

ফনা করা, A. *v.* To destroy.

ফন্দী, A. *n.* A snare, a plot, a scheme.

ফন্দীবাজ, A. *n.* A plotter, a schemer. *adj.* Plotting, scheming.

ফন্দী খাটান, A. *v.* To devise a scheme, to plot.

ফম—*See* ফহম.

ফয়েজ, A. *n.* Liberality, bounty, charity.

ফয়সলা, A. *n.* A decree, settlement, judgment. (Also written ফয়সালা).

ফয়সলা করা, A. *v.* To settle, to decide, to judge.

ফয়সলানামা, A. *n.* A decree, an award.

ফরক, A. *n.* Difference ; interval ; distance. *adj.* Different, separate.

ফরক করা, A. *v.* To separate ; to distinguish.

ফর্কাণ—*See* ফুর্কাণ.

ফরজ, A. *e.* A divine decree or command : an incumbent duty ; a supposition.

ফরজ করা, A. *v.* To take for granted.

ফরজী, A. *adj.* Incumbent, obligatory ; suppositious.

ফরজন্দ, P. *n.* A son ; a descendant.

ফরমান, P. *n.* A royal mandate ; an order, a charge, an edict ; a charter.

ফরমানবরদার, P. *adj.* Obedient, subject to, compliant. *n.* A servant.

ফরমানবরদারী, P. *n.* Subordination, obedience, fealty.

ফরমানা, P. *v.* To issue an order, to declare. *n.* An order, a command.

ফরমায়েশ, P. *n.* Order, command ; requisition.

ফরমায়েশী, P. *adj.* Relating to a command, made to order.

ফররুখ, P. *adj.* Happy, fortunate.

ফরশ, P. *n.* A carpet ; a bed ; a pavement.

ফররাশ, P. *n.* A servant whose duty it is to spread carpets.

ফরাখুর, P. *adj.* Worthy, fit.

ফরাখুশী, P. *n.* A pleasant countenance.

ফরাগৎ, A. *n.* Leisure, cessation from labour, respite, ease, comfort. (Also written ফরাকৎ).

ফরাজী, A. *n.* The name of a Muslim sect.

ফরায়েজ, A. *n.* Muhammadan obligatory religious duties ; the Muslim law of inheritance and partition of property. (Also written ফরাজ).

ফরাশ—*See* ফরশ.

ফরিয়াদ, P. *n.* A complaint ; a suit.

ফরিয়াদ করা, P. *v.* To complain.

ফরিয়াদী, P. *n.* A complainant, a plaintiff.

ফরীক, A. *n.* A section, division; a party (to a suit).

ফরীকা, A. *n.* A large party of men; an army, a troop.

ফরীদ, A. *n.* A gem; a Muslim saint. *adj.* Unique.

ফরোখৎ, P. *n.* Sale, disposal.

ফরোখৎ করা, P. *v.* To sell.

ফর্দ্দ, (A. ফরদ). *n.* An inventory, a list; a single individual. *adj.* Single.

ফলানা, (A. ফুলান). *n.* Such an one, so-and-so.

ফলীতা, (A. ফতীলা) *n.* A wick, a fuse.

ফসক, A. *n.* Sin; adultery.

ফসল, A. *n.* A section, a division; a crop, a harvest.

ফসলী, A. *adj.* Pertaining to the crops. The *Fasli* era which began in Sep. 1555.

ফসাদ, A. *n.* Sedition, intrigue; contention; corruptness, violence; war.

ফসাদী, A. *adj.* Depraved; mutinous.

ফসাহৎ, A. *n.* Pure language; eloquence.

ফহম, A. *n.* Understanding; sense.

ফাকা, A. *n.* Poverty, want.

ফাজিল, A. *n.* Excess, overplus, balance; a learned man. *adj.* Superfluous; learned, distinguished; worthless, talkative.

ফাজিল বাকী, A. *n.* Balance in favour.

ফাজিল বাকী করা, A. *v.* To strike a balance.

ফাজিলাৎ, A. *n.* Balances, surpluses. (*Plu.* of ফাজিল).

ফাটক, H. A prison.

ফাৎওয়া—*See* ফৎওয়া.

ফাতেহা, A. *n.* The name of the opening chapter of the Quran.

ফাতেহা পড়া, A. *v.* To read prayers over the dead.

ফাতেহা দেওয়া, A. *v.* To make offerings to saints with prayers.

ফানী, A. *adj.* Transitory, fleeting; mortal.

ফানুস, A. *n.* A lantern, a lamp, a light-house.

ফায়েজ, A. *n.* Bounty, favour.

ফায়সলা—*See* ফয়সলা.

ফায়েদা, A. *n.* Benefit, profit, advantage.

বে-ফায়েদা. *adv.* In vain, fruitlessly.

ফায়েল, A. *n.* An agent, a doer.

ফারখৎ, A. *n.* A bill of divorcement; a deed of acquittance, a dissolution of partnership.

ফারখতী, A. *n.* A release, a discharge, *adj.* Released, discharged.

ফারশী, P. *n.* The Persian language.

ফারাক—*See* ফরক.

ফারাজ—*See* ফরায়েজ.

ফারেগ, A. *adj.* Free, discharged, disengaged; empty.

ফালতু, H. *adj.* Spare, surplus; useless, unemployed, unnecessary.

ফাশ, P. *adj.* Apparent, manifest; disclosed.

ফাশ করা, P. *v.* To divulge, to display.

ফাসেক, A. *n.* A sinner, a fornicator. *adj.* Sinful, depraved.

ফিকর, A *n.* Thought, reflection, anxiety; device, means. (Sometimes written ফিকির).

ফিকর করা, A. *v.* To ponder, to reflect; to contrive; to plot.

ফিকরী, A. *adj.* Anxious, solicitous.

ফিকা, (A. ফিকহ্). *n.* Muhammadan ecclesiastical law; jurisprudence.

ফিতর, A. *n.* Breaking of the fast *Ramadhan*; alms distributed on that occasion. ইদ-উল্‌-ফিতর, the breaking the fast festival of *Ramadhan*.

ফিৎনা, A. *n.* Sedition, revolt: evil.

ফিৎরৎ, A. *n.* Nature; wisdom; plot.

ফিৎরতা, A. *adj.* Natural.

ফিদা, A. *n.* Sacrifice; devotion, ransom. *adj.* Devoted to.

ফিদা করা, A. *v.* To ransom.

ফিদীয়ৎ, A. *n.* Ransom, redemption.

ফিরকা, A. *n.* A tribe; a sect, a class.

ফিরার হওয়া, A. *v.* To flee, to run away; to abscond.

ফিরারী, A. *adj.* Fugitive, absconded. *n.* A fugitive; a cultivator who abandons his lands and absconds.

ফিরারী জমী, land which has been abandoned by an absconding tenant.

ফিরাশ—*See* ফরাশ.

ফিহ্‌রিস্ত, P. *n.* A list, a catalogue: a table of contents.

ফী, A. *Pre.* In, each, every, *per*, as ফী বিগাহ, *per bigha*.

ফীরোজা, P. *n.* A turquoise; *adj.* Blue.

ফীল, A. *n.* An elephant.

ফীল-খানা, A. *n.* Elephant sheds.

ফুকার—*See* পুকার.

ফুফু, *n.* Maternal aunt.

ফুরকাণ, A. *n.* The Quran; that which distinguishes between right and wrong, hence the Old Testament is, in the Quran, called *Furqan*.

ফুরসৎ, A. *n.* Opportunity, leisure.

ফুরুজ, A. *n.* Portions, shares.

ফুলান—*See* ফলানা.

ফুস্‌লানা, H. *v.* To coax, to entice.

ফুস্‌লানী, H. *n.* Coaxing, enticement.

ফেকা, H. *v.* To throw, to fling.

ফের, H. *adv.* Again, afterwards.

ফেরৎ দেওয়া, H. *v.* To return, to give back.

ফেরদৌস, P. *n.* Heaven, paradise.

ফেরীব, P. *n.* Deception, fraud, trick.

ফেরীব দেওয়া, P. *v.* To cheat, to deceive.

ফেরীববাজ, P. *n.* A cheat, a deceiver.

ফেরীববাজী, P. *n.* Fraud, deceit.

ফেরীবী, P. *adj.* Deceitful, fraudulent.

ফেরেস্তা, (P. ফেরেশ্‌তা). *n.* An angel.

ফেরোজ—*See* ফীরোজ.

ফেলজামিন, A. *n.* Security for good behaviour; a bond binding one to keep the peace.

ফেলশানী, A. *n.* Prostitution, adultery.

ফেসাদ—*See* ফসাদ.

ফৈজৎ—*See* ফজীহৎ.

ফোতা, P. *n.* Taxes, revenue.

ফোতাখানা, P. *n.* A treasury.

ফোয়ারা, A. *n.* A fountain, a spring.

ফৌক, A. *adj.* Above. *n.* Summit; loftiness.

ফৌকিয়ৎ, A. *n.* Pre-eminence.

ফৌজ, A. *n.* An army, a multitude. A police jurisdiction.

মুক্তি ফৌজ, The Salvation army.

ফৌজদার, A. *n.* An officer of police or soldiers. [to a police officer.

ফৌজদারী, A. *adj.* Criminal; relating

ফৌজদারী আদালৎ, a criminal court.

ফৌজদারী, করা, A. *v.* To commit a criminal offence.

ফৌজী, A. *adj.* Military.

ফৌৎ, P. *n.* Death.

ফৌৎজমী, P. *n.* Land which cannot be identified, though shown on the rent-roll.

ফৌতী, P. *adj.* Deceased, dead. *n.* A deceased person; the property of a deceased who dies intestate.

ফৌতিক, *n.* Perquisites; something given or obtained above the regular salary.

ব

বি, P. Used in compounds to signify with, by, according to, as ব-মাল, found in possession of (stolen) property; বকলম, (written) with a pen.

বঃ, An abbreviation for বকলম

বকর, A. *n.* A cow.

বকর-ঈদ, the cow festival, or feast of sacrifice, which forms part of the ceremonies of the great Meccan pilgrimage.

বকরা, H. *n.* A male goat.

বকরী, H. *n.* A female goat.

বকলম, A. *adv.* (Written) with a pen; (Used when the signature of an illiterate person is written by a second person.)

বকেয়া, A. *n.* Arrears, dues; surplus balances; remainder. *adj.* Old.

বকেয়া হাল, Current balances.

বকেয়া বাকী, Arrears on previous year's rent.

বকো, *n.* A journey.

বক্ত—*See* ওক্ত.

বখৎ, P. *n.* Lot, fortune, luck.

বখতাবর, (P. বখতাওর), *adj.* Fortunate, lucky.

বখতাবরী, P. *n.* Good fortune, prosperity.

বখরা, P. *n.* A share, a dividend, distribution: allotment.

বখরা করা, P. *v.* To divide, to share, to assign. [sharer.

বখরাদার, P. *n.* A shareholder, a

বখশ, P. *n.* Pardon; a gift.

বখশ দেওয়া, P. *v.* To give: to forgive.

বখশা, P. *v.* To give; to forgive.

বখশিশ, P. *n.* A gift, a present, a reward, a gratuity.

বখশিশনামা, P. *n.* A deed of gift.

বখশী, P. *n.* The pay-master of Muhammadan armies.

বখীল, A. *adj.* Covetous, miserly, *n.* A miser.

বখীলী, A. *n.* Covetousness, miserliness.

বগল, P. *n.* The armpit ; the side.

বগলী, P. *n.* A purse, a small bag.

বটওয়ারা, H. *n.* A share, a division ; partition.

বজরা, H. A pleasure-boat, a house-boat ; a *budgerow*.

বজা, P. *adj.* Just, true, valid, suitable, proper. *adv.* Fitly, properly.

বজা রাখা, P. *v.* To perform, to give effect to, to comply with, to carry through.

বজ্জাৎ, (P. বদ্‌জাৎ). *adj.* Baseborn, vile, wicked.

বজ্জাতী, P. *n.* Wickedness ; lowness of birth.

বতন, A. *n.* The womb ; the belly.

বতারীখ A. *adv.* On the date, dated.

বদ, P. *adj.* Bad, evil. (Often used as a prefix as বদবখৎ, unlucky).

বদখৎ, P. *adj.* Writing a bad hand.

বদখো, P. *adj.* Malevolent, evil.

বদকার, P. *adj.* Evil, licentious.

বদখেয়াল, P. *n.* A bad intention.

বদখেয়ালী, P. *adj.* Having a bad intention, evil-intentioned.

বদতর, P. *adj.* Worse.

বদদোয়া, P. *n.* An imprecation, a curse.

বদনজর, P. *n.* Envy. *adj.* Envious.

বদন, A. *n.* The body, the trunk.

বদনাম, P. *n.* An evil name, a bad reputation.

বদনিয়ৎ, P. *adj.* Having a bad intention.

বদবখৎ, P. *adj.* Unlucky, unfortunate.

বদবো, P. *n.* An evil smell, a stink.

বদমাশ, A. *n.* A rogue, a scoundrel. (Sometimes written বদমাইশ).

বদমাশী, A. *n.* Bad livelihood, villany, wickedness.

বদমেজাজ, A. *n.* Bad character.

বদর, A. *n.* The full moon.

বদরাহ, A. *n.* An evil source of life. *adj.* Disorderly, taking a bad path.

বদল, A. *n.* Exchange, transfer ; substitute ; change, alteration.

বদল করা, A. *v.* To change, to exchange, to alter.

বদলাই, A. *n.* Something given in exchange. (Often written বদলী).

বদলান, A. *v.* To change, to alter.

বদলাবদলী, A. *n.* Interchange, barter.

বদলী, A. *n.* Exchange ; a substitute, a transfer.

বদলী হওয়া, A. *v.* To be transferred.

বদলী করা, A. *v.* To transfer ; to change.

বদলে, A. *adv.* Instead of, in place of.

বদস্ত, P. *adv.* By hand.

বদহজম, P. *n.* Indigestion.

বদহাল, P. *n.* Poor circumstances, poverty.

বনা, H. *n.* A fabrication, a machination. *adj.* Made, finished.

বনায়া, H. *adj.* Made, composed.

বনাম, P. *adv.* In the name of ; *alias.*

বনি, A. *n.* Sons, children.

বনিয়াদ—*See* বুনিয়াদ.

বন্দ, P. *n.* A fastening, a knot, a bandage, a joint ; an embankment ; a plot, a piece.

বন্দ করা, P. *v.* To confine, to enclose, to stop, to frustrate.

বন্দখানা, P. *n.* A jail.

বন্দর, P. *n.* A port, a harbour.

বন্দা, P. *n.* A slave, a servant ; a human being. Also used as a term of humility when speaking of oneself.

বন্দিগী, (P. বন্দগী). *n.* Worship ; service ; salutation. *Int.* Bravo ! thanks ! farewell !

বন্দিগী করা, P. *v.* To worship, to serve.

বন্দী, P. *n.* A prisoner ; a slave-girl, a female servant, (Generally written বাঁদী for slave-girl.)

বন্দুক, T. *n.* A gun, a musket.

বন্দে, P. *n.* A plot of land.

বন্দেশ, P. *n.* A tying, an invention, a contrivance. (Also written বন্দেজ).

বন্দোবস্ত, P. *n.* A settlement, a plan ; a method, an arrangement.

বমাল, P. *adv.* With (stolen) property ; (Said of one found in possession of stolen property).

বয়—*See* বায়.

বয়াদ,—*See* বাদ.

বয়ান, A. *n.* An explanation, a declaration ; a report.

বয়ান করা, A. *v.* To declare, to express ; to describe, to relate.

বয়াবান, P. *n.* A desert, a wilderness.

বয়াসৎ, A. *n.* A mission.

বয়েৎ—*See* বায়েৎ.

বরকৎ, A. *n.* A blessing, a benediction ; prosperity, good-fortune.

বরকন্দাজ, P. *n.* A rifleman ; a messenger ; a watchman ; an escort.

বরখাস্ত, P. *n.* Removal, dismissal, recall ; breaking up of a court of justice, adjournment.

বরখাস্ত করা, P. *v.* To dismiss ; to adjourn.

বরখেলাফ, P. *adj.* Contrary, opposite, inconsistent, untrue.

বরখেলাফী, P. *n.* Opposition.

বরগজীদা, P. *adj.* Selected, chosen.

বরগা, H. *n.* A rafter.

বরজ, A. *n.* A *pan*-garden.

বরজখ, A. *n.* The interval between death and the resurrection in Muslim theology.

বরতন, H. *n.* A vessel, a dish.

বরতরফ P. *adj.* Removed, dismissed. *n.* Dismissal, discharge.

বরদা, T. *n.* A slave ; a captive.

বরদার, P. *n.* A bearer, a carrier. (Often used in compounds, as আসা-বরদার, a mace-bearer.)

বরদাস্ত, (P. বরদাশ্‌ৎ). *n.* Endurance, forbearance, patience.

বরহক, A. *adj.* Right, proper rightful.

বরফ, P. *n.* Ice, snow.

বরফী, H. *n.* A kind of sweetmeat.

বরবাদ, P. *adj.* Wasted, lost, ruined. *n.* Wastage, destruction.

বরবাদ করা, P. *v.* To destroy.

বরাৎ, P. *n.* A multitude, assembly; a commission, a warrant, an assignment, a letter of reference; fortune, fate; necessity.

শব-ই-বরাৎ, P. *n.* The night of record in which men's deeds for the coming year are said to be written down.

বরাতী, P. *adj.* Relating to a warrant. H. A marriage procession; one who joins in a marriage procession.

বরাবর, P. *adj.* Even; like; smooth; accurate; up to; exactly. *adv.* Continually, throughout.

বরাদ্দ, P. *n.* Something that is fixed; an estimate. *adj.* Fixed.

বরাদ্দ করা, P. *v.* To estimate.

বরামদ, P. *n.* Accusation, impeachment; issue. [vilify.

বরামদ করা, P. *v.* To accuse, to

বল্‌কে, P. *Con.* Moreover, but, even, on the other hand.

বলন্দ, P. *adj.* High. (Sometimes written বুলন্দ.)

বলাগৎ, A. *n.* Eloquence, rhetoric.

বশর, A. *n.* A man, a human being.

বশারৎ, A. *n.* Good news; revelation.

বশীর, A. *n.* A bearer of good news; an evangelist.

বস,—*See* বাস.

বসীরৎ, A. *n.* Perception, discernment.

বস্তা, P. *n.* A package, a bundle, a parcel.

বস্তাবন্দী, P. *n.* The making up a parcel; baling.

বহন, H. *n.* A sister.

বহর, A. *n.* Width; a fleet of boats; the sea, the ocean.

বহরী, A. *adj.* Relating to the sea, maritime.

বহম-- *See* বাহেম.

বহানা, P. *n.* Pretence, excuse, apology; feint, stratagem; means.

বহার, P. *n.* Spring; beauty, verdure.

বহাল, A. *adj.* Happy, prosperous; confirmed, re-instated; upheld.

বহাল করা, A. *n.* To engage; to confirm; to re-instate.

বহুৎ, H. *adj.* Much, great, many; sufficient. *adv.* Greatly.

বাঁঝা, H. *adj.* Barren, childless.

বাইল, H. *n.* An ox, a bullock.

বাউরা, *adj.* Insane, mad.

বাকী, A. *adj.* Remaining; eternal (as opposed to ফানী transitory). *n.* Arrears; the remainder; a balance.

বাকী কৈফিয়ৎ, a statement of outstanding balances.

বাকী মালগুজারী, arrears of revenue.

বাকীদার, A. *n.* One in arrears.

বাকীয়াৎ, A. *n.* Balances, arrears.

বাগ, P. *n.* A garden, an orchard.

বাগবান, P. *n.* A gardener.

বাগবানী, P. *n.* The occupation of a gardener.

বাগাৎ, P. *n.* Gardens, orchards. *adj.* Garden (land).

বাগী, P. *adj.* Disloyal, seditious, mutinous. *n.* A rebel, an insurgent.

বাগীছা, P. *n.* A small garden.

বাজ, P. A particle affixed to nouns, denoting agent, doer, proficient in; a hawk. *adv.* Again, back.

বাজ রাখা, P. *v.* To detain, to withhold, to confine; to prohibit.

বাজ বহা, P. *v.* To abstain from, to shun, to withdraw; to give up.

বাজার, P. *n.* A market, a fair, a bazar.

বাজারে, P. *adj.* Commonplace, public; ready-made.

বাজার করা, P. *v.* To go shopping.

বাজী, P. *n.* A stake, a wager; a game, sport, exhibition, trick, fire-works.

বাজী করা, P. *v.* To defeat, to beat.

বাজী লাগা, P. *v.* To gamble, to bet.

বাজীকর, P. *n.* One who performs tricks, a juggler; one who prepares fire-works.

বাজীগার—Same as বাজীকর.

বাজু, P. *n.* An arm; a wing; an ornament for the arm.

বাজুবন্দ, P. *n.* An ornament for the arm.

বাজে, A. *adj.* Some, certain; incidental, useless, unprofitable.

বাজে কথা, useless talk;

বাজে জমীন, land not subject to taxes, because useless.

বাজে খরচ, contingent or incidental expenses.

বাজে লোক, an outsider, an extra man.

বাজেয়াপ্ত, *adj.* Forfeited, deducted, confiscated

বাজেয়াপ্ত করা, *v.* To forfeit, to escheat; to proscribe.

বাটওয়ারা—*See* বটওয়ারা.

বাট্টা, H. *n.* Rate of exchange.

বাৎ, H. *n.* A word.

বাৎচিৎ, H. *n.* Conversation.

বাত্লান, H. *v.* To tell, to inform, to publish.

বাতাশা, P. *n.* A kind of sweetmeat.

বাতিন, A. The inside; the mind, the heart; disposition.

বাতিনী, A. *adj.* Interior, private, internal; hidden, esoteric

বাতিল, A. *adj.* False; null, abolished, useless.

বাদ, P. *n.* Air, wind. (A. বয়াদ) *adv.* After, afterwards. *n.* A deduction.

বাদ দেওয়া, A. *v.* To deduct; to exclude.

বাদবান, P. *n.* A sail.

বাদল, H. A cloud, rain.

বাদশাহ্, P. *n.* A king, a sovereign.

বাদশাহ জাদা, P. *n.* A prince.

বাদশাহৎ, P. *n.* Kingdom, sovereignty.

বাদশাহী, P. *adj.* Royal, state.

বাদা, P. *n.* A desert, a forest.

বাদাম, P. *n.* An almond; a sail

বাদামী, P. *adj.* Of the shape or colour of an almond.

বান, P. A suffix signifying keeper as দরবান, a door-keeper.

বানু, P. *n.* A lady, a woman.

বান্দা—*See* বন্দা.

বাফ্‌তা, P. *n.* A kind of cloth, half silk, half cotton.

বাব, A. *n.* A door ; a chapter, a section ; a matter, a subject.

বাবৎ, A. *n.* An item, an account, an article : a business, an affair. *adv.* On account of, relating to, respecting, for. (Sometimes written বাবদ and বাবুদ.)

বাবরছী, T. *n.* A cook.

বাবরছীখানা, T. *n.* A kitchen.

বাবা, P. *n.* Father.

বাবু, P. (?) *n.* A title of respect, as Sir, Mr. ; a gentleman.

বাবুয়ানা, P. Foppery, dandyism.

বাবুগিরী, P. Foppery ; putting on the airs of a babu.

বায়, A. *n.* Sale, buying and selling.

বায়ৎ, A. *n.* The initiation of a disciple, pledging fealty to a spiritual leader ; a couplet, a verse ; a house as বায়ৎ-উল্-মাল, a treasury, বায়ৎ-উল্-মুকদ্দস, Jerusalem.

বায়না, A. *n.* Earnest money, advance payment.

বায়নানামা, A. *n.* A contract entered into on payment of earnest money.

বায়নামা, A. *n.* A deed of sale ; a deed of conveyance.

বায়ী, A. *n.* A seller.

বার, P. *n.* A load, a burden.

বারদেগর, P. *adv.* Another time ; again.

বারবরদার, P. *n.* A porter, a carrier.

বারবরদারী, P. *n.* Transport, carriage.

বারান্দা, (P. বরামদা). *n.* A verandah, a porch.

বারী, A *n.* The Creator, God.

বারীতালা, A. *n.* The most high God.

বারুদ, P. *n.* Gunpowder.

বালগ, A. *adj.* Of age, one who has reached puberty.

সাবালগ, of age.

নাবালগ, under age.

বালা, P. *adj.* High, exalted. *adv.* On, above.

বালাই, A. *n.* A calamity, misfortune, distress, difficulty.

বালাখানা, P. *n.* An upper room ; a balcony.

বালাপোশ, P. *n.* A coverlet, a quilt a cloth covering for the head.

বালিশ, P. *n.* A cushion, a pillow.

বাশিন্দা, P. *n.* A resident, an inhabitant, a dweller.

বাস, (P. বাজ). *Int.* Enough ! hold stop !

বাস্ত জমী, *n.* Homestead land.

বাহাদুর, (P. বহাদুর) *adj.* Brave, bold *n.* A hero, a champion ; a title of honour conferred by the Indian government.

বাহাদুরী, P. *n.* Valour, courage expertness ; ostentatious display

বাহানা—*See* বহানা.

বাহার—*See* বহার.

বাহাল—*See* বহাল.

বাহেস, (A. বহস). *n.* Debate, discussion, dispute.

বাহেস করা, A. *v.* To debate, discuss.

বিওয়া, H. *n.* A widow.

বিচে, H. *adv.* Beneath.

বিছ, H. *adj.* Between, among. *n.* Middle, centre.

বিজলী, H. *n.* Lightning. [captial.

বিজারৎ, A. *n.* Agency, commission ;

বিতারীখ—*See* বতারীখ.

বিদয়ৎ, A. *n.* Innovation ; schism, heresy. (Often written বেদাৎ.)

বিদয়তী, A. *n.* An innovator in religion, a schismatic.

বিন্, A. *n.* A son (From ইবন).

বিন্‌ৎ, A. *n.* A daughter.

বিনা, A. *n.* A foundation, source, basis ; beginning.

বিবী—*See* বীবী.

বিমা—*See* বীমা.

বিয়াজ, H. *n.* Interest on money.

বিয়াজখোর, H. *n.* A usurer.

বিয়ান, H. *n.* Early morning.

বিরাদর, P. *n.* A brother ; a relation.

বিরাদরী, P. *n.* Brotherhood, fraternity.

বিল্‌কুল, A. *adj.* Whole, entire ; all. *adv.* Wholly, entirely.

বিলমাজ্‌মা, P. *adv.* On the whole ; in the aggregate.

বিলা, A. *prep.* Without (*i.e.* not having) as বিলা শক. without doubt, বিলা শর্‌ৎ, unconditional.

বিলাৎ, A. *n.* A country ; a foreign country ; England. (Probably derived from the Arabic *Walayat*).

বিলাৎ বরাৎ, A. *n.* The assignment of monies owing to one to a second person.

বিলাতী, A. *adj.* Belonging or pertaining to *Bilat* : European, British.

বিল্লা, H. *n.* A male cat.

বিল্লী, H. *n.* A female cat.

বিস্‌মিল্লা, A. In the name of God. (বে+ইসম্+আল্লা).

বীবী, P. *n.* A lady, a matron ; a wife.

বীবীজান, P. *n.* A term of respectful address to Muslim ladies.

বীবীআনা, P. *adj.* Belonging to or fit for a lady. *n.* Putting on the airs of a lady.

বীমা, P. *n.* Insurance.

বীমা করা, P. *v.* To insure.

বীমাই ছিঠি. P. *n.* An insurance policy.

বীমার, P. *adj.* Sick, unwell.

বীমারী, P. *n.* Sickness, disease. (In Bengali these words are often transposed, and বীমার is used as a noun, whilst বীমারী becomes an adjective. The word is often written বেমার.)

বীরাণ, (P. ওইরাণ). *adj.* Waste, uncultivated.

বীরাণ করা, P. *a.* To destroy, to lay waste.

বীরাণা, P. *n.* Forest land, a waste.

বুখার, A. *n.* Steam ; fever ; anger, sorrow.

বুগজ, A. *n.* Malice, hatred, resentment.

বুজুর্গ, P. *adj.* Great, distinguished, noble, revered, respected ; aged. *n.* A respectable person, a wise man : an old man.

বুজুর্গী, P. *n.* Greatness, honour ; dignity, rank.

বুৎ, P. *n.* An image, an idol.

বুৎপরস্ত, P. *n.* An idolater.

বুৎপরস্তী, P. *n.* Idolatry.

বুনিয়াদ, P. *n.* Foundation, basis.

বুনিয়াদী, P. *adj.* Having a good foundation ; relating to the foundation, fundamental.

বুর্কা, A. *n.* A veil, a dress covering the whole head and body with small eye-holes through which to see.

বুর্মা, P. *n.* A gimlet, a bit.

বুর্হান, A. *n.* Proof, demonstration.

বুরা, H. *adj.* Bad, wicked ; ugly, base, worthless.

বুরাক, A. *n.* The steed on which Muhammad is alleged to have ascended to heaven.

বুরুজ, A. *n.* A tower ; a cable ; a lunar mansion ; a constellation.

বুলন্দ, A. *adj.* High.

বুলন্দী, A. *n.* Height.

বুলবুল্, A. *n.* The nightingale.

বুলূগ, A. *n.* Maturity ; being of age.

বে, P. A prefix meaning contrary to, without (*ie.* not having), corresponding with the English un, im, non, &c. as বে-দরদ, painless. বে-তাল, disordered, বে-ইমান, faithless.

বে-ওফা, A. *adj.* False, faithless.

বেওয়া—*See* বিওয়া.

বেওরা, H. *n.* A detailed account, a narrative : intelligence.

বে-আইন, A. *adj.* Illegal, contrary to law.

বে-আকেল, A. *adj.* Thoughtless, foolish.

বে-আদব, A. *adj.* Ill-mannered, rude.

বে-আদবী, A. *n.* Rudeness, bad manners.

বে-আন্দাজ, P. *adj.* Immoderate, unlimited.

বে-আন্দাজী, P. *n.* Immoderateness.

বে-আব্রু, P. *adj.* Dishonourable ; disgraced.

বে-আবাদ, P. *adj.* Uncultivated.

বে-আয়েব, A. *adj.* Flawless, perfect, sinless.

বে-ইজ্জৎ, P. *adj.* Without honour, disgraced.

বে-ইন্সাফ, A. *adj.* Unjust.

বে-ইমান, A. *adj.* Unbelieving, faithless ; irreligious.

বে-ওকুফ, A. *adj.* Foolish, ignorant, thoughtless. (Sometimes written বে ওয়াকিফ.)

বে-ওকুফী, A. *n.* Thoughtlessness, foolishness, ignorance.

বে-ওজর, A. *adj.* Without excuse, inexcusable.

বে-ওয়ারিস, A. *adj.* Without heirs.

বে-করার, A. *adj.* Restless.

বে-করারী, A. *n.* Restlessness.

বে-কসুর, A. *adj.* Blameless, faultless, acquitted.

বে-কায়েদা, A. *adj.* Disarranged, disorderly, irregular.

বে-কার, P. *adj.* Unemployed, idle, worthless.

বে-কুব—*See* বে-ওকুফ.

বেগ, T. *n.* A title of Moghul gentlemen.

বে-গতিক, P. *adj.* Helpless.

বেগম, T. *n.* A Muhammadan princess, a title of a Moghul lady.

বেগর, A. *Pre.* Without, with the exception of, except.

বেগানা, P. *adj.* Strange, foreign. *n.* A stranger, a foreigner.

বেগার, P. *n.* Forced labour, impressment.

বেগার ধরা, P. *v.* To impress, to take forced service.

বেগারী, P. *n.* The impressment of labour without remuneration.

বেগারে, P. *adj.* Working without remuneration.

বে-গুনাহ্, P. *adj.* Sinless, innocent.

বে-চারা. P. *adj.* Without a remedy, helpless. *n.* A helpless person.

বে-জা, P. *adj.* Out of place, improper, unlawful, wrong.

বেজাই, A. *adj.* Very, much. P. *adv.* Instead of, in place of.

বেজার, P. *adj.* Angry, displeased, vexed, grieved.

বে-জারী, P. *adj.* Uncommon, not current.

বেটা, H. *n.* A son.

বেটী, H. *n.* A daughter.

বে-তমীজ, A. *adj.* Undiscerning ; rude, indiscreet.

বেতর, P. *adj.* Unusual, uncommon ; ill-behaved.

বে-তরফ, A. *adj.* Of no party, impartial.

বে-তস্‌দীক, A. *adv.* Under one's own signature ; in witness of.

বে-তার, P. *adj.* Agitated, impatient.

বে-তারীখ, A. *adv.* Under date ; dated.

বে-তাল, P. *adj.* Disordered.

বে-দখল, A. *adj.* Not included in, not comprised under ; put out of possession, ousted.

বে-দখল করা, A. *v.* To dislodge, to oust, to disturb one's possession of.

বে-দখলী, A. *n.* Exclusion, deprivation, dispossession, ejectment.

বে-দম, P. *adj.* Breathless. *adv.* Unceasingly.

বে-দলীল, A. *adj.* Without proof ; not having any documentary proof.

বেদাৎ—*See* বিদ্‌য়ৎ.

বে-দীন, A. *adj.* Irreligious.

বে-নমাজী, P. *n.* One who does not say the Muhammadan ritual prayers.

বে-নাম, P. *adj.* Transferred to another name ; anonymous ; a fictitious name.

বে-নামদার, P. *n.* The holder of property actually belonging to another.

বে-নামী, P. *adj.* (Property) in another's name than the real owner ; anonymous.

বে-নামী করা, P. *v.* To transfer property to the name of another.

বে-পরওয়া, P. *adj.* Free of care ; fearless.

বে-পরওয়াই, P. *n.* Fearlessness, carelessness.

বে-পর্দা, P. *adj.* Without a curtain, shameless, exposed.

বে-ফায়েদা, A. *adj.* Unprofitable, vain.

বে-ফিকর, A. *adj.* Thoughtless, heedless.

বে-বাক, P. *adj.* All, the whole ; even ; paid up. *adv.* Wholly, fully.

বে-বাক করা, P. *v.* To pay up in full, to settle.

বেমার—*See* বীমার.

বে-মালিক, A. *adj.* Without an owner.

বে-মালুম, A. *adj.* Ignorant, unacquainted with, unaware.

বে-মাহুল, A. *adj.* Free from taxes or postage.

বেয়াকুব—*See* বে-ওকুফ.

বেয়াবান—*See* বয়াবান.

বেরাম, A. *n.* Disease, sickness. (From বে-আরাম.)

বেরাদর—*See* বিরাদর.

বেল্‌কুল—*See* বিল্‌কুল.

বেলমোক্তা, P. *adj.* Approximate, inexact.

বেলমোক্তা পাট্টা, a lease which is given for land without proper measurement, and for a limited time.

বে-লিহাজ, A. *adj.* Shameless.

বে-লিহাজী, A. *n.* Shamelessness.

বেলোয়ারী, P. *adj.* Made of glass.

বেশ, P. *adj.* Superior, excellent, good. *int.* Good ! well done ! bravo !

বে-শক, A. *adv.* Undoubtedly, without doubt ; certainly.

বে-শরম, P. *adj.* Shameless.

বেশাৎ, P. *n.* Stock, capital.

বেশাতী, P. *n.* A small shop-keeper.

বেশী, P. *n.* Excess, increase. *adj.* Much, many ; too much, too many, more.

বে-শুমার, P. *adj.* Countless, numberless, without calculation.

বে-সওয়ার, P. *adj.* Riderless.

বে-সবব, A. *adj.* Without cause.

বে-সবর, A. *adj.* Impatient.

বে-সরা, A. *adj.* Out of turn ; improper, unusual.

বে-সুদ, P. *adj.* Without interest.

বেহতর, P. *adj.* Better, superior, more worthy.

বেহতরী, P. *n.* Advantage, welfare, virtue.

বে-হদ্দ, A. *adj.* Boundless, unlimited ; immoderate. *adv.* Vastly exceedingly.

বে-হায়া, P. *adj.* Shameless, immodest.

বে-হাল, A. *adj.* Wretched, miserable.

বে-হাসিল, A. *adj.* Unproductive, fruitless ; non-dutiable.

বে-হুরমৎ, A. *adj.* Void of honour.

বেহুদা, P. *adj.* Senseless, foolish ; absurd.

বে-হুশ, P. *adj.* Without understanding ; senseless, stupified.

বে-হুশইয়ার—Corruption of বে-হুশ.

বেহেস্ত, (P. বেহেশ্‌ৎ). *n.* Paradise, heaven.

বৈঠক, H. *n.* A sitting, a session,

বৈঠকখানা, H. *n.* A sitting room ; a reception room.

বৈয়ৎ—*See* বায়ৎ.

বোচা, T. *n.* A bundle, a package.

ব্যামোহ্‌, *n.* Illness, affliction.

ভ

ভর, H. *adj.* Used in compounds to signify full of, as far as, up to, whole, as জিন্দাগীভর for the whole period of life. (Sometimes written ভোর).

ভরপুর, H. *adj.* Full, overflowing.

ভরাতী জমী, A. *n.* New land formed by deposits from the river.

ভাগজোৎ পাট্টা, *n.* A deed under which the tenant returns one half the produce in lieu of rent.

ভাগবিলী পাট্টা—Same as ভাগজোৎ পাট্টা.

ভাগা, H. *v.* To flee.

ভাঝ করা, H. *n.* Pleating (in tailoring.)

ভাতিজা, H. *n* Nephew, brother's son.

ভাতিজী, H. *n.* Niece, brother's daughter.

ভান, P. *n.* Plea, pretext, pretence, sham ; excuse.

ভান করা, P. *v.* To pretend.

ভায়া, H. *n.* A brother.

ভিশ্‌টা, H. *n.* Filth, excrement.

ভিস্তী, P. *n.* A water-carrier.

ভী, H. *conj.* Also, besides.

ভূক, H. *n.* Hunger ; appetite.

ভূকা, H. *adj.* Hungry ; longing for

ভেট, H. *n.* A meeting, an interview.

ভেটা, H. *v.* To meet, to encounter.

ভেজা, H. *v.* To send.

ভেজাল, *n.* Adulteration ; trouble.

ভেজাল দেওয়া, *v.* To adulterate.

ভোগদখল, A. *n.* Possession, use.

ভোগদখল করা, A. *v.* To enjoy all the rights of possession.

ভোর—*See* ভর.

ম

মওলা—*See* মৌলা.

মক্‌দম্—*See* মুকদ্দম.

মক্‌দুমা, A. A title of respect. (*corr.* of মুকদ্দমা).

মকদ্দমা—*See* মুকদ্দমা

মক্‌দুর, A. *n.* Power, ability.

মকবুল, A. *adj.* Accepted, received ; chosen : agreeable.

মকর, A. *n.* Deceit, pretence, imposture.

মকর করা, A. *v.* To pretend, to feign.

মকর্‌ররী,—*See* মুকর্‌রর্.

মক্‌রূহ, A. *adj.* Disgusting, loathsome, hateful.

মকশ—*See* মশক.

মকসদ, A. *n.* Purpose, intention, end.

মকসুম, A. *adj.* Divided, partitioned.

মকান, A. *n.* A place : a room, a dwelling-house.

মকানদার, P. *n.* An owner, a householder.

মকাম, A. *n.* A place, a site ; an opportunity ; a halt.

মকামী, A. *adj.* Relating to a place.

মক্কার, A. *n.* A cheat, an impostor.

মক্কেল, (A. মুয়াক্কেল). *n.* A client.

মখ্‌দুম, A. *n.* A master ; a Muslim priest.

মখ্‌মল, A. *n.* Velvet.

মখ্‌লুক, A. *adj.* Created.

মখ্‌লুকাৎ, A. *n.* Creation ; created things.

মগজ, P. *n* The brain ; the pith or kernel of anything ; pride.

মগজী, P. *n.* A border, edge, rim.

মগজী লাগান, P. *n.* Running and felling (in tailoring).

মগজী সেলাই, P. *n.* Hemming.

মগ্‌ফুর, A. *adj.* Forgiven.

মগরেব, A. *n.* The west ; sunset ; the fourth of the Muslim liturgical prayers said at sunset.

মগরূর, A. *adj.* Proud, arrogant. (Sometimes written মগরা.)

মগরূরী, A. *n.* Pride.

মগলূব, A. *adj.* Defeated, overcome.

মগলূব করা, A. *v.* To defeat.

মজকুর, A. *adj.* Aforesaid, mentioned.

মজকুরী, A. *n.* Process-serving, notice, the contents of a written statement.

মজদুর, A. *n.* A labourer, a porter.

মজবুৎ, A. *adj.* Firm, strong, durable.

মজবুতী, A. *n.* Firmness strength.

মজবুর করা, A. *v.* To constrain, to compel.

মজমুন, A. *n.* Contents, substance, purport.

মজমুয়া, A. *n.* A collection, an assembly: a total.

মজরিম—*See* **মুজরিম**.

মজলিস, A. *n.* A meeting, an assembly.

মজলিস-খানা, A. *n.* A place of meeting; a hall, a synagogue.

মজলুম, A. *adj.* Oppressed, injured.

মজহব, A. *n.* A religion: a sect; a school of Muhammadan jurisprudence.

মজহবী, A. *adj.* Religious: relating to a sect or school of jurisprudence.

মজহর—*See* **মুজহির**.

মজা, P. *n.* Flavour; a joke.

মজা করা, P. *v.* To make a joke; to enjoy.

মজাদার, P. *adj.* Witty, humerous.

মজাদারী, P. *n.* Wittiness.

মজাজ—*See* **মেজাজ**.

মজাকিয়া, P. *adj.* Fond of joking, witty, playful.

মজাল, A. *n.* Authority, power, ability.

মজীদ, A. *adj.* Noble, great, glorious.

মজুৎ—*See* **মৌজুদ**.

মজুমদার, P. *n.* Formerly a keeper of revenue accounts under Muslim administration, now a family surname.

মজুর, (P. **মজদুর**). *n.* A day-labourer.

মজুরদার, P. *adj.* Subsisting by labour.

মজুরী, (P. **মজদুরী**). *n.* Wages, hire, pay; the work of a day-labourer.

মজুস, A. *n.* A Magian, a Parsee.

মঞ্জিল, A. *n.* A stage of a journey; a storey of a house; a dwelling, an inn.

মঞ্জিলৎ, A. *n.* Station, dignity.

মঞ্জুর, A. *adj.* Granted, sanctioned, admitted, assented to: looked at.

মঞ্জুর করা, A. *v.* To approve, to sanction, to grant.

মঞ্জুরী, A. *n.* Assent, approval, sanction.

মৎ, H. *adv.* Do not, do'nt.

মতন, A. *n.* The text of a book or deed.

মৎওয়ালা, H. *adj.* Drunken. excited.

মৎলব, A. *n.* Wish, desire; purpose, intention.

মৎলবী, A. *adj.* Having a certain desire; selfish.

মৎলববাজ *Same as* মৎলবী.

মতাবেক *See* মুতাবেক.

মতালিক *See* মুতয়াল্লিক.

মতালেব. A. *n.* Demands. requests. desires. (*Plu.* of মৎলব.)

মদ্দা. A. *n.* A diacritical sign in Arabic script.

মদদ্, A. *n.* Help. assistance.

মদদ্‌গার. A. *adj.* Helping. giving assistance. *n.* A helper. a benefactor.

মদার, A. *n.* An orbit. a circle ; a place of retirement.

মনক্কা, A. *n.* Stoned raisins.

মন্‌কির, —*See* মুন্‌কির.

মন্‌কজী, A. *adj.* Elapsed, expired. *n.* Arrears. [dignity.

মন্‌সব, A. *n.* An office, a post ; a

মন্‌সবদার. A. *n.* An officer : a magistrate.

মন্‌সবদারী. A. *n.* The occupation of a *mansab* ; an official position.

মন্‌সুখ, A. *adj.* Repealed, abolished.

মন্‌সুব, A. *adj.* Placed, appointed. constituted, determined. established.

মন্‌সুবা, A. *n.* A contrivance, plan : intention. determination. [dent.

মন্‌সুবাবাজ. A. *adj.* Sagacious ; pru·

মনাজাৎ—*See* মুনাজাৎ.

মনাসেব—*See* মুনাসিব.

মনীব—*See* মুনীব.

মফ্‌কুদ, A. *adj.* Missing, lost.

মফস্বল, (A. মুফস্‌সল). *n.* The country as opposed to the town, the *moffussil* ; the inside as opposed to the outside ; total. *adj.* Distinct, clear ; detailed.

মব্‌লগ, A. *n.* Total. the whole : a sum of money : a place of arrival.

মব্‌লগে. A. *adv.* On the whole.

মবলগবন্দী. A. *n.* The total in written words.

মবারক—*See* মুবারক. [dispensed with.

ময়াজুর, A. *adj.* Forgiven. excused ;

ময়দা, P. *n.* Flour.

ময়দান, A. *n.* A plain, a meadow, a park. ten মা.)

ময়া. A. *pre.* With. (Also writ-

ময়াজ আল্লা, A. *int.* I take refuge with God ! God forbid !

মরওয়ারীদ, P. *n.* Pearls.

মর্‌কুম, A. *adj.* Written. [tioned.

মর্‌কুমা, A. *adj.* Aforesaid, men

মর্‌জী, A. *n.* Assent ; choice, wish.

মর্‌জী সে, A. *adv.* Voluntarily.

মর্তবান, A. *n.* A glazed jar.

মর্তবাহ, A. *n.* Rank : time (বার).

মরদ. P. *n.* A man ; a male ; a husband : a human being. (Sometimes written মর্দ্দা.)

মর্‌দানা, P. *adj.* Male, manly, masculine.

মর্‌দানী. P *n.* Manliness.

মর্‌দূদ. A. *adj.* Rejected. excluded. *n.* A reprobate.

মর্‌মর্. P. *n.* Marble.

মরসিয়া, A. *n.* A funeral oration.

মরসুম, A. *adj.* Usual. customary. *n.* A time. a season.

মরহবা, A. *int.* Welcome ! Bravo !

মর্‌হুম. A. *adj.* A recipient of God's mercy ; dead ; 'the late.' (The word is written after the name of a deceased person.)

মরাতেব, A. *n.* Dignities honours.

মরিচা —*See* মুরচা.

মলকহ, A. *n.* Quickness of perception, intellect.

মলঊন, A. Accursed: excommunicated. (Sometimes written মালাউন.)

মলম, ('P. মরহম). *n.* Salve. ointment.

মলামৎ, A. *n.* Reproach, reproof.

মলায়েম—*See* মুলায়েম.

মশক, A. *n.* Practice. exercise. (Sometimes written মকশ). P. Musk; a leathern bag; the skin of an animal used as a bag for carrying water.

মশক্কৎ, A. *n.* Labour: trouble, difficulty.

মশগুল. A. *adj.* Engaged. busy, employed.

মশ্‌রূৎ, A. *adj.* Stipulated, agreed, conditional.

মশহুর. A. *adj.* Celebrated. known, famous.

মশাল, P. *n.* A torch.

মশালচী, P. *n.* A torch bearer: a kitchen assistant, a scullion.

মশাহরা, A. *n.* Salary. stipend.

মশিয়ৎ, A. *n.* Will, power.

মস্‌কন, A. *n.* A dwelling.

মসখরা, A. *adj.* Jocular, droll. *n.* A jester, a joker.

মসখরা করা, A. *v.* To jest, to joke.

মস্‌খামী, A. *n.* Joking, fun.

মসজিদ, A. *n.* A mosque, a *masjid.*

মস্‌হফ, A. *n.* A book: the Quran.

মস্ত, P. *adj.* Intoxicated, excited. *must.*

মস্তয়াদ—*See* মুস্তায়েদ.

মসনদ, A. *n.* A cushion, a seat, a throne.

মসল. A. *n.* A proverb, a maxim.

মসলন্দ. P. *n.* A throne; a mat.

মসলহৎ. A. *n.* Expedience; consultation.

মসলহৎ করা, A. *v.* To consult together.

মসলা, A. *n.* An example.

মসালা. A. *n.* Spices, ingredients: materials; a maxim, an aphorism; a tenet; a proposition.

মসীবৎ—*See* মুসীবৎ.

মসীহ. A. *n.* The Messiah, Christ.

মস্তানী. P. *n.* Drunkenness, intoxication.

মস্তী, P. *n.* Drunkenness; ecstasy.

মহকুমা, A. *n.* A sub-division of a district; the jurisdiction of a sub-divisional officer.

মহতাব, P. *n.* The moon: moonlight.

মহদী—*See* মাহদী.

মহফুজ, A. *adj.* Protected, guarded, safe.

মহবুব, A. *adj.* Beloved.

মহব্বৎ, A. *n.* Love, friendship.

মহমুদ. A. *adj.* Praised.

মহর. A. *n.* A marriage portion a dowry. (See further under মোহর.)

মহরনামা, A. *n.* A deed of settlement.

মহরাণা, A. *n.* A marriage fee paid to the celebrant.

মহর্‌রম—*See* মোহররম.

মহরী—*See* মুহরীর.

মহরম, A. *n.* A confidant; a consort; one within the prohibited degrees of marriage.

মহ্রূম, A. *adj.* Excluded, deprived.

মহল, A. *n.* A place, a quarter; a halting-place; a building; an opportunity; a district, an estate; a department. (Sometimes written মহাল or মাহাল.)

মহলৎ, A. *n.* Delay, respite; time.

মহলদার, A. *n.* A land-owner; a zemindar.

মহলদারী, A. *n.* Land-ownership.

মহলা, A. *n.* A storey of a building.

মহলুফ, A. *adj.* Sworn.

মহল্লা, A. *n.* A district or quarter of a town; a ward.

মহল্লাদার, A. *n.* An officer in charge of a *mahalla*.

মহসিল, A. *n.* A tax-collector; a bailiff.

মহ্সুল, A. *n.* Taxes, customs, excise. *adj.* Collected.

মহসুলদার, A. *n.* A collector of taxes or fines.

মহাকেজ—*See* মুহাকেজ.

মহাবেরা—*See* মুহাবেরা.

মহাল, A. *n.* Real or landed estate.

মহাসিল, A. *n.* Produce, profit.

মাওরা, H. *n.* Leaven; starch.

মাওলানা—*See* মৌলানা.

মাঃ—An abbreviation of মারফৎ.

মাং—An abbreviation of মারফৎ.

মাকুল, (A. মক্কুল). *adj.* Suitable, proper, right, worthy, good.

মাখুজ, A. *adj.* Involved, implicated.

মাখুজ করা, A. *v.* To incriminate, to bring to trial.

মাখুজী, A. *n.* Arrest.

মাঙ্গা, H. *v.* To ask, to pray.

দোয়া মাঙ্গা, to pray, to supplicate.

মাঙ্গনীবন্দ, H. *adj.* Betrothed.

মাজরা, A. *n.* An event, an incident.

মাজুর A. *n.* A kind of sweetmeat.

মাজুজ, A. *n.* Magog. A tribe of Central Asia mentioned in the Quran. (*See* under ইয়াজুজ.)

মাজুল, A. *adj.* Deposed, dismissed.

মাজেজা, A. *n.* A miracle, (*Esp.* one wrought by a prophet. c.f. কিরামৎ.)

মাতব্বর, (A. মুয়াতেবর). *n.* A chief, a leader; a mediator. *adj.* Chief, principal.

মাতব্বরী, A. *n.* Leadership.

মাতম, A. *n.* Mourning; *esp.* the mourning at the Mohurram festival.

মাতমদার, A. *n.* A mourner.

মাতোয়ালা, H. *adj.* Intoxicated.

মাদর, P. *n.* Mother.

মাদা, P. *n.* A female. *adj.* Feminine. (Also written মাদী).

মাদইয়ান, P. *n.* A mare.

মানা, A. *n.* A hindrance, prohibition; objection.

মানা করা, A. *v.* To forbid; to hinder,

মানিন্দ, A. *adj.* Like.

মানে, A. *n.* Meaning, purport.

মানোই, A. *adj.* Pertaining to the meaning.

মাপ—*See* মাফ.

মাফ, (A. মুয়াফ). *n.* Forgiveness, pardon; excuse. *adj.* Forgiven; excused.

মাফ করা, A. *v.* To forgive; to excuse.

মাফিক—*See* মুয়াফিক.

মাফী, A. *n.* Forgiveness.

মাফীদার, A. *n.* A holder of rent-free land.

মাবুদ, A. *adj.* Worshipped, adored, *n.* God.

মামলা, (A. মুয়ামলা). *n.* A law-suit, litigation ; an affair, a business.

মামলা করা, A. *n.* To engage in litigation.

মামলাদার, A. *n.* A litigant.

মামলাবাজ, A. *adj.* Litigious.

মামু, H. *n.* A maternal uncle.

মামুল, A. *n.* A custom ; usage, practice [current.

মামুলী, A. *adj.* Customary, usual,

মামুলী আদায়, A. *n.* Rent which is paid in kind.

মায়েল, A. *adj.* Inclined ; partial ; bent.

মায়ী, A. *adj.* Established, fixed.

মারফৎ, (A. মরারিফৎ). *n.* Knowledge ; revelation ; *prep.* Through, by, by means of.

মারফৎদার, A. *n.* An agent.

মারাকেল্লা, A. *n.* A complete victory.

মারসেকেল্লা, A. *n.* A complete victory.

মারহাবা—*See* মরহবা.

মাল, A. *n.* Property, goods, capital.

মালখানা, A. *n.* A store-room ; a treasury.

মালগুজার, A. *n.* One who pays rent or tribute.

মালগুজারী, A. *n.* Land revenue, rent ; revenue assessment.

মালগাড়ী, A. *n.* A railway train, a goods train.

মালজামিন, A. *n.* Security for property.

মালদার, A. *adj.* Wealthy, possessing property.

মালদারী, A. *n.* Wealth, opulence.

মাল-মক্রুকা, A. *n.* Distrained property.

মালমত্তা, A. *n.* Goods, property, chattels ; revenue.

মাল-আমুওয়াৎ, A. *n.* Property left by a deceased person.

মালাই, (P. বালাই). *n.* Cream.

মালাউন—*See* মলয়ুন.

মালাক, A. *n.* An angel.

মালাম, A. *n.* Wrestling.

মালামৎ—*See* মলামৎ.

মালায়েক, A. *n.* Angels.

মালিক, A. *n.* Owner, propietor. master, king.

মালিকী, A. *n.* Ownership, royalty.

মালিকী স্বত্ব, A. *n.* Proprietary rights.

মালিকীয়ৎ, A. *n.* Ownership.

মালিকানা, A. *n.* Rent paid to a zamindar by a *patnidar* ; compensation given to one who has been deprived of land. *adj.* Proprietary ; as মালিকানা স্বত্ব, proprietary rights.

মালিশ, P. *n.* A rubbing, polish.

মালিশ করা, P. *v.* To rub, to polish.

মালীয়ৎ, A. *n.* Wealth ; value.

মালের জমী, A. *n.* Land upon which rent is payable.

মাল্লা, (A. মল্লাহ). *n.* A sailor, a boatman.

মালুম, A. *adj.* Known, perceived, experienced.

মাশুক, A. *n.* One beloved, a sweetheart, a lover.

মাশুর—*See* মশহুর.

মাসরা—*See* মুশাহরা.

মাস্থম, A. *adj.* Innocent, sinless, protected. *n.* An infant.

মাসুল, A. *n.*, Tribute, duty, any fee on letters, goods etc.

মাহ, P. *n.* The moon ; a month.

মাহদী, A. *n.* One rightly guided : the twelfth *Imam* or successor to Ali. The *Mahdi*.

মাহাল—*See* মহল.

মাহিনা, (P. মাহিয়ানা). *n.* A month, monthly wages, salary.

মাহিনাদার, P. *adj.* Receiving monthly wages. *n.* A servant.

মাহিয়ানা, P. *adj.* Monthly, *n.* Salary, wages.

মিকদার, A. *n.* A quantity, a measure, the sum total, amount.

মিছিল—*See* মিসল.

মিজরাব, A. *n.* That which is placed on the finger and by which a zither string is played.

মিজাজ—*See* মেজাজ.

মিজান—*See* মীজান.

মিনতি, (A. মিন্নৎ). *n.* Entreaty, supplication, importunity.

মিনতি করা, A. *v.* To entreat, to supplicate.

মিনা,—*See* মীনা.

মিম্বর, (A. মিন্বর). *n.* A mosque pulpit.

মিয়া, P. *n.* A Muhammadan gentleman. *int.* Sir, Mr.

মিয়াদ—*See* মেয়াদ.

মিয়ানা, P. *n.* A palanquin.

মিরধা, P. *n.* An overseer ; a headman.

মিরাজ—*See* মেরাজ.

মিল্‌ক, A. *n.* Landed property : rent free land, possession, mastership.

মিল্‌কী, A. *adj.* Proprietary.

মিলাপ, H. *n.* Social conversation : reconciliation.

মিলাপ রাখা, H. *v.* To agree with, to be reconciled to.

মিস্‌ওয়াক, A. *n.* A piece of stick used as a tooth-brush.

মিস্‌কীন, A. *n.* A pauper, a poor man. *adj.* Poor ; meek, mild.

মিস্‌মার, A. *adj.* Demolished, broken.

মিস্‌রী, A. *n.* Sugar-candy.

মিসল, A. *n.* Like, similar. *n.* The papers or records of a case.

মিসাল, A. *n.* Likeness, similitude : example.

মিসিল, A. *n.* A procession ; an assembly. (Often written মিছিল.)

মিহনৎ—*See* মেহনৎ.

মিহ্‌রাব, A. *n.* An arch ; the alcove in a mosque which points the direction to Mecca ; a covering ; a scaffolding. (Sometimes written মেরাপ.)

মিহীন, P. *adj.* Fine, delicate, thin.

মীজান, A. *n.* A balance, a pair of scales.

মীনা, P. *n.* A goblet ; the heavens ; enamel. H. Rain, water.

মীনাকার, P. *n.* An enameller.

মীনারা, A. *n.* A pillar, a *minaret*, a tower.

মীয়াদ, A. *n.* Imprisonment ; time, turn ; period, duration. (Sometimes written মেয়াদ.)

মীয়াদ কাটা, A. *v.* To serve a term of imprisonment.

মীয়াদ দেওয়া, A. *v.* To imprison. to send to jail.

মীয়াদী, A. *adj.* Imprisoned : conditional : terminable. for a limited period.

মীয়াদী পাট্টা. a lease granted for a limited period

মীয়াদী জমা. A. *n.* Land held under a lease which is not permanent, but only for a limited period.

মীর, A. *n.* A chief. a leader : a Muhammadan title.

মীর্জা, P. *n.* The son of a chief. *adj.* Noble, highborn.

মীর্জাই, P. *n.* A kind of waist coat.

মীরাস, A. *n.* Inheritance : an hereditary estate ; a bequest.

মীরাসী, A. *adj.* Inherited.

মুওয়ক্কেল- *See* মক্কেল.

মুওয়জ্জফ, A. *n.* A fixed salary.

মুওয়াখের, A. *adj.* Last, rearmost.

মুওয়াজ্জা. A. *n.* A turning towards ; standing face to face.

মুকদ্দম, A. *adj.* Antecedent, prior : superior *n.* The head man of a village.

মুকদ্দমা, A. *n.* A law-suit ; a preamble, an introduction.

মুকদ্দমা করা. A. *v.* To engage in a law-suit.

মুকম্মল, A. *adj.* Perfect. complete.

মুকররর্, A. *adj.* Fixed. established : determined.

মুকররী, A. *adj.* Relating to what is fixed, a tenure held at a fixed rental.

মুকররী পাট্টা. A. *n.* A permanent lease.

মুকররী ইস্তিমরারী. a tenure the rental of which is only fixed for the life of the holder.

মুকাবেল. A. *adj.* Opposite. confronting : like.

মুকাবেলা. A. *n.* Comparison : opposition : meeting. a coming face to face. *adv.* Before.

মুকাবেলা করা. A. *n.* To meet face to face, to interview. to confront : to oppose.

মুকির, A. *n.* Confession.

মুকির হওয়া, A. *v.* To confess.

মুখ্তসর. A. *adj.* Abridged. concise. *n.* An abstract, an abridgement.

মুখ্তার, A. *n.* An agent. a delegate ; an attorney. a solicitor practising in the lower courts. (Sometimes written মোক্তার.)

আম-মুখ্তার. A general agent.

খোদ-মুখ্তার. One who does his own business. *adj.* Independant.

মুখ্তার-নাম', A. *n.* A power of attorney. a document investing one with authority to act as an agent. [a *mukh'ar*.

মুখ্তারী. A. *n.* The profession of

মুখ্তারী করা. A. *v.* To practise the profession of a *mukhtar*.

মুখবির, A. *n.* An attesting witness to a deed.

মুখলিস. A. *adj.* Sincere.

মুখাতিব. A. *n.* One who addresses another. [turn towards.

মুখাতিব হওয়া, A. *v.* To address, to

মুখালিফ, A. *n.* An opponent, an adversary, *adj.* Opposed to, contrary to.

মুখালিফৎ, A. *n.* Enmity, opposition.

মুচদ্দী—*See* মুসদ্দী.

মুচলেকা, T. *n.* Recognizance, a bond.

মুজ্‌তাহিদ, A. *n.* A spiritual leader; a Muslim jurist.

মুজরা, A. *n.* A deduction, an allowance, a remission.

মুজরা দেওয়া, A. *v.* To make a reduction, to make a rebate; to give credit for.

মুজ্‌রিম, A. *n.* A sinner; a criminal.

মুজহির, A. *n.* An informer.

মুজাফ, A. *adj.* Added, increased.

মুজাফৎ, A. *n.* Addition.

মুজাহিম, A. *n.* An obstacle, a hindrance. *adj.* Forbidden: hindering.

মুজাহিমদার, A. *n.* An objector, a claimant.

মুজিব, A. *n.* Cause, reason, motive.

মুজিবাৎ, A. *n.* Motives, grounds.

মুড়ি সেলাই, H. *n.* Hemming.

মুতফর্‌রক, A. *adj.* Scattered, divided; different, miscellaneous.

মুতবর্‌রক, A. *adj.* Blessed: heavenly.

মুতয়াল্লিক, A. *adj.* Hanging on, connected with, attached to, appertaining to.

মুতয়ায়েন, A. *adj.* Appointed, constituted.

মুতয়াল্লী, A. *n.* A trustee of a Muhammadan religious endowment.

মুতসদ্দী, A. *n.* A manager, a superintendent; a writer, a clerk.

মুত্তকী, A. *adj.* Pious, devout.

মুতা, A. *n.* Temporary marriage allowed by the Shiahs.

মুতাবেক, A. *adv.* According to, in conformity with.

মুতাবেকৎ, A. *n.* Conformity, accordance.

মুতাবেক হওয়া, A. *v.* To agree, to correspond to, to coincide with.

মুতী, A. *adj.* Subject to, obedient.

মুতর্জ্জিম, A. *n.* A translator.

মুদাম, A. *adv.* Always, for ever.

মুদামী, A. *adj.* Permanent.

মুদাফৎ, A. *n.* Addition, appendage; a suburb.

মুদী, H. *n.* A grocer.

মুদীখানা, A. *n.* A grocer's shop.

মুদ্দৎ, A. *n.* A space of time, term, period, duration.

মুদ্দতী, A. *adj.* Temporary.

মুদ্দা, A. *n.* Object, scope; wish.

মুদ্দায়ী, A. *n.* A plaintiff, a prosecutor; a claimant, an informant.

মুদার্‌রিস, A. *n.* A teacher, a professor.

মুদ্দালেহ, A. *n.* A defendant. (A corruption of মুদ্দায়ী আলায়হে)

মুন্‌কির, A. *n.* One who denies, an athiest, a defendant in a suit. The name of an angel who is supposed to examine the dead in the tomb.

মুন্‌কির হওয়া, A. *v.* To deny, to renounce.

মুন্‌তজের, A. *adj.* Expectant, waiting.

মুন্‌শী, A. *n.* A writer, a secretary; a teacher; a title of respect.

মুন্‌শীগিরী, A. *n.* The occupation of a *munshi*; a clerkship: a teachership.

মুন্‌শীয়ানা, A. *n.* The skill of a *munshi.*

মুন্‌শীখানা. A. *n.* A vernacular record-room.

মুনসেফ, P. *n.* A subordinate civil judge, a *munsif.*

মুনসেফী, P. *n.* Justice, equity.

মুনসেফী করা, P. *v.* To execute justice, to preside over a court of justice.

মুনসেরীম, A. *n.* Manager; head [clerk.

মুনাজাৎ, A. *n.* Prayers, supplications.

মুনাজাৎ করা. A. *n.* To supplicate, to entreat.

মুনাদী. A. *n.* A proclamation.

মুনাজেরা, A. *n.* Disputation, discussion, debate.

মুনাফা, A. *n.* Profits, gains.

মুনাফিক, A. *n.* A hypocrite.

মুনাসেব, A. *adj.* Fit, suitable, proper.

মুনাসেব হওয়া. A. *v.* To apply to, to suit.

মুনীব, A. *n.* Master, lord.

মুনীর, A. *adj.* Bright.

মুফৎ, A. *adj.* Gratuitous, gratis.

মুফৎ খোরা. A. *adv.* Gratuitously.

মুফতী. A. *n.* A Muhammadan lawyer or judge.

মুফলিস, A. *adj.* Penniless, indigent. *n.* A pauper.

মুফলিসী, A. *n.* Poverty; pauperism.

মুফস্সল—*See* মফস্বল.

মুফস্সের, A. *n.* A commentator, an exegete.

মুফীদ, A. *adj.* Good, beneficial.

মুবতদা, A. *n.* The subject of a sentence.

মুবাজী. (A. মুওয়াজী). *n.* Sum, total.

মুবাদেলা, A. *n.* Exchange, interchange, transfer.

মুবারক, A. *adj.* Blessed; fortunate.

মুবারকী, A. *n.* Blessedness, happiness.

মুবাহেসা, A. *n.* Discussion, debate.

মুমতাজ, A. *adj.* Exalted, eminent, illustrious.

মুমতাজ করা. A. *v.* To exalt.

মুমানী, H. *n.* An aunt, a mother's brother's wife.

মুমিন—*See* মোমিন.

মুয়াজ্জমা, A. *adj.* Great, exalted. (*Esp.* used of Mecca.)

মুয়াজ্জিন, A. *n.* The one who calls to Muslim prayers; a *muazzin.*

মুয়াজেজা—*See* মাজেজা.

মুয়াফিক, A. *adj.* Corresponding to, fit, suitable, like. (Sometimes written মাফিক).

মুয়াফিকৎ, A. *n.* Fitness; correspondence, likeness.

মুয়াল্লা, A. *adj.* High, exalted.

মুয়াল্লেম. A. *n.* A teacher.

মুর. *n.* Myrrh. *adj.* Bitter.

মুরগ, P. *n.* A cock.

মুরগী, P. *n.* A hen.

মুরতদ. A. *n.* A renegade, an apostate.

মুরতদ হওয়া. A. *v.* To apostatise.

মুরত্তব, A. *adj.* Arranged; put in order.

মুর্দার, P. *adj.* Dead; unlawful. *n.* A dead body.

মুর্দারফরাশ, P. *n.* One who carries the dead.

মুরব্বা, A. *n.* Preserved fruit: pickles

মুরব্বী, A. *n.* A teacher; a protector, a patron: a head man.

মুরব্বীগিরী, A. *n.* Teachership, patronage.

মুরশিদ, A. *n.* A guide, an instructor, a spiritual preceptor.

মুরাকেবা, A. *n.* Contemplation.

মুরাদ, A. *n.* Request; wish, intention; object; tenor, tendency: a vow.

মুরাফা, A. *n.* An appeal (in law).

মুরীদ, A. *n.* A disciple, a pupil. *adj.* Desirous.

মুলতবী, (A. মুলতওয়ী). *adj.* Deferred, delayed, postponed; pending.

মুলতবী রাখা, A. *v.* To postpone, to defer, to suspend.

মুলাকাৎ, A. *n.* A meeting, a visit; carnal intercourse.

মুলাকাতী, A. *n.* A visitor, an acquaintance.

মুলায়েম, A. *adj.* Soft, tender; moderate.

মুলাহেজা, A. *n.* Inspection; notice, regard; examination. *adj.* Seen, compared, examined.

মুলাহেজা করা, A. *v.* To consider, to examine; to notice.

মুলুক, A. *n.* Country, region.

মুল্লা, A. *n.* A religious preceptor a priest; a school-master.

মুশকুকৎ—*See* মশকুকৎ.

মুশকিল, A. *n.* A difficulty, perplexity, trouble.

মুশখসা, A. *adj.* Ascertained, stipulated, fixed, estimated.

মুশতহর, A. *adj.* Proclaimed, made public.

মুশতহর করা, A. *v.* To proclaim, to advertise.

মুশরিক, A. *n.* A polytheist, an idolater; the East.

মুশাবা, A. *adj.* Like, resembling.

মুশাবিহৎ, A. *n.* Likeness.

মুশাহরা, A. *n.* Salary, stipend.

মুশাহিদা, A. *n.* Sight, vision: observation.

মুসদ্দী—*See* মতসদ্দী.

মুসন্নিফ, A. *n.* A writer, an author.

মুসব্বর, A. *n.* Aloes

মুসম্মাৎ, A. *n.* A title prefixed to the names of Muhammadan ladies: *adj.* Called.

মুসলমান, A. *n.* A follower of the Muhammadan religion, a Mussulman.

মুসলমানী, A. *n.* Circumcision. *adj* Pertaining to the Muhammadan religion.

মুসলমানী করা, A. *v.* To circumcise.

মুসল্লা, A. *n.* A carpet on which prayer is made; a place of prayer.

মুসল্লী, A. *n.* One who prays.

মুসল্লম, A. *adj.* Entire, sound, whole; admitted. (Sometimes written মছলম.)

মুসলিম, A. *n.* A follower of Islam, a Muslim.

মুসলেকা—*See* মুচলেকা.

মুসাফের, A. *n.* A traveller.

মুসাফেরখানা, A. *n.* An inn a place for accommodating travellers.

মুসাবিদা, (A. মসওদা). *n.* A draft, a rough sketch.

মুসাবিদা করা, A. *v.* To make a rough draft of a document.

মুসাহেব, A. *n.* A companion, an associate, a friend.

মুসীবৎ, A. *n.* Misfortune, trouble, difficulty.

মুস্তকীম, A. *adj.* Erect ; straight.

মুস্তফা, P. *adj.* Chosen, selected.

মুস্তৈদ, A. *adj.* Ready, prepared ; capable.

মুস্তাজির, A. *n.* A farmer, a contractor, a lessee.

মুস্তাজিরী. A. *n.* A lease of land, a holding ; a contract.

মুস্তাহিল, P. *adj.* Cheerful.

মুহকম. A. *adj.* Strong, strengthened. *adv.* Firmly.

মুহ্তাজ. A. *adj.* Poor, needy ; defective.

মুহাদ্দস, A. *n.* One well-versed in the traditions. A traditionist

মুহরির, (A মুহর্রির). *n.* A writer, a clerk ; an accountant.

মুহরিরগিরী, A. *n.* The occupation of a clerk.

মুহস্সেল, A. *n.* A bailiff, a tax-collector.

মুহাজরী, A. *n.* Appearing against, sueing anyone.

মুহাজের. A. *n.* An emigrant ; one who flees a country for the sake of religion. *Esp.* a title of those who fled with Muhammad from Mecca to Medina.

মুহাজেরৎ, A. *n.* Emigration.

মুহাফেজ, A. *n.* A record-keeper ; a watchman, a guard.

মুহাফেজখানা, A. *n.* A record room.

মুহাফেজৎ, A *n.* Guardianship, protection.

মুহাবরা, A. *n.* Practice, usage, idiom.

মুহাসেল, A. *n.* Produce, profits, proceeds.

মুহিব. A. *n.* A friend, a lover.

মুহিম. A. *adj.* Important, great *n.* A feat, an exploit.

মুটিয়া. H. *n.* A porter, a cooly.

মুর্চা. P. *n.* Rust ; a rampart.

মুরীস, A. *n.* A legator ; one from whom a legaey is derived.

মেওয়া, P. *n.* Fruit. *adj.* Fruitful, sweet.

মেকরাজ, P. *n.* A pair of scissors shears.

মেকরান, P. *v.* To deceive.

মেখ. P. *n.* A plug : a nail, a pin

মেখী. P. *adj.* Counterfeit ; a coin plugged with base metal.

মেজ, P. *n.* A table

মেজ লাগান. P. *v.* To lay the table.

মেজাজ, A. *n.* Nature, temperament. disposition ; pride.

মেজাজী, A. *adj.* Proud ; of a certain temper.

মেজাজদার, A. *adj.* Proud, conceited.

মেথর, (P. মেহ্তর). *n.* A sweeper, a scavenger, a *methar*.

মেথরানী, P. *n.* A female sweeper.

মেদা. (P. মাদা). *adj.* Slow, dull, stupid.

মেদামারা. P. *adj.* Dull lifeless.

মেয়াদ—*See* মীয়াদ.

মেয়ানা, P *adj.* Middling, moderate.

মেরাজ, A. *n.* The alleged ascension of Muhammad to heaven during his lifetime.

মেরাজ করা, A. *v.* To ascend to heaven.

মেরামৎ, (A. মরম্মৎ). *n.* Repairs : amendment.

মেরামৎ করা, A. *v.* To repair.

মেহনৎ, A. *n.* Labour, exertion ; care.

মেহনৎ করা, A. *v.* To labour, to exert oneself.

মেহনতানা, A. *n.* Wages : payment for services rendered.

মেহনতী, A. *adj.* Laborious, industrious : painstaking. *n.* A labourer.

মেহমান, P. *n.* A guest ; a stranger.

মেহমানখানা, P. *n.* A house or room for the reception of guests.

মেহমানদার, P. *n.* A host.

মেহমানদারী, P. *n.* Hospitality.

মেহমানী, P. *n.* A feast.

মেহ্‌রাব—*See* মিহ্‌রাব.

মেহের, P. *n.* Kindness, favour, mercy.

মেহেরবান, P. *adj.* Kind, merciful, gracious.

মেহেরবানী, P. *n.* Kindness, favour.

মেহেরবানী করা, P. *v.* To have mercy upon ; to do a favour to.

মোকররী—*See* মুকর্‌রী.

মোকাবেলা—*See* মুকাবেলা.

মোকাম, (A. মকাম). *n.* Address, residence ; a place.

মোক্তার—*See* মুখ্‌তার.

মোগল, P. *n.* A Moghul : a class of Muhammadans.

মোজা, P. *n.* A sock, a stocking.

মোট, H. *n.* A load, a burden.

মোবারক—*See* মুবারক.

মোম, P. *n.* Beeswax.

মোমজামা, P. *n.* Wax-cloth.

মোমবাতী, P. *n.* A wax-candle.

মোমিন, A. *n.* A believer, a Muslim.

মোয়াজী—*See* মুবাজী.

মোয়াহেদ, A. *n.* A Unitarian ; a believer in the unity of God.

মোরগ—*See* মুরগ.

মোলায়েম—*See* মুলায়েম.

মোহররম, A. *adj.* Sacred, prohibited ; the name of the first month of the Muhammadan year ; the name of the great Shiah festival *Moharrem.*

মোহর, P. *n.* A seal ; a gold coin. (See further under মহর).

মোহরী—*See* মুহুরির.

মোহাদ্দিস—*See* মুহদ্দিস.

মৌকা, A. *n.* A place ; an opportunity.

মৌকুফ, A. *adj.* Stopped, suspended, relinquished ; excused ; abolished, dismissed. *n.* Liberation, release.

মৌকুফ করা, A. *v.* To discontinue, to suspend ; to remove from office ; to abolish ; to remit, to excuse.

মৌকুফ রসদ, A. *n.* Rent of land, the collection of which is suspended for a stated period.

মৌকুফ হাজৎ—Same as মৌকুফ রসদ.

মৌজ, A. *n.* A wave ; emotion, ecstasy.

মৌজ মারা, A. *v.* To be thrilled with ecstasy ; to enjoy oneself.

মৌজা, A. *n.* A place ; a village ; a district containing a number of villages.

মৌজুদ, A. *adj.* Existing, present, ready; in stock; balance. (Also written মজুৎ and মজুদ.)

মৌজুদ তহবীল, A. *n.* Cash in hand.

মৌজুয়া, A. *n.* Subject, topic.

মৌজেব—*See* মুজিব.

মৌৎ, A. *n.* Death.

মৌতাৎ, P. *n.* An artificial craving or appetite.

মৌরূস, A. *adj.* Inherited; permanent. *n.* Heritable right; an inherited property carrying right of permanent occupancy.

মৌরুসী, A. *adj.* Hereditary; permanent.

মৌরুসী পাট্টা, An hereditary lease carrying right of permanent occupancy at a fixed rental.

মৌলবী, A. *n.* A Muhammadan priest, a *Maulvi.*

মৌলা, P. *n.* Master; Lord, God.

মৌলানা, P. *n.* A learned Muhammadan; a spiritual leader.

মৌলুদ, A. *adj.* Born. *n.* The celebration of the anniversary of Muhammad's birth.

মৌসিম, A. *n.* Season; time.

মৌসিমী, A. *adj.* Seasonable; in season.

মৌসুফ, A. *adj.* Described; celebrated; before-mentioned.

র

রইস—*See* রয়ীস.

রওনক—*See* রৌনক.

রওব—*See* রয়ব.

রওয়াক, A. *n.* A masonry bench in front of a house; a verandah, a porch; a tent. (Sometimes pronounced রগ্).

রওয়াজ, A. *adj.* Usual, customary. *n.* Usage, custom.

রওয়ানা, P. *n.* A despatching; a departure; a pass a passport.

রওয়ানা হওয়া, P. *v.* To depart, to set out.

রওয়ানা করা, P. *v.* To despatch, to send.

রওয়ায়েৎ—*See* রিওয়ায়ৎ.

রক, T. *n.* A masonry bench in front of a house. (Sometimes pronounced রগ্, *See* রওয়াক from which it is probably derived.)

রকন—*See* রুকন.

রকবা, A. *n.* An area; the land comprised in a village measurement.

রকম, A. *n.* Kind, sort, manner; amount.

রকাৎ, A. *n.* A bowing in prayer, genuflection; a portion of a chapter from the Quran; one complete repetition of the Muslim liturgical prayers.

রগ্, P. *n.* A sinew. (See further under রক).

রগবৎ, A. *n.* Inclination, disposition.

রজক, A. *n.* Daily food, subsistence. (Also written রিজক.)

রজব, A. *n.* *Rajab,* the name of the seventh month of the Muhammadan year.

রজয়াৎ, A. *n.* Receiving back a divorced wife.

রজা, A. *n.* Consent, acquiescence; pleasure; leave.

রজামন্দ, A. *adj.* Willing, consenting.

রজামন্দী, A. *n.* Consent; satisfaction.

রজ্জাক, A. *n.* A provider; one of the names of God.

রদ, A. *n.* Refutation; abrogation, rejection; the surplus of an estate after the legal portions have been distributed among the heirs.

রদ করা, A. *v.* To refute; to abrogate, to cancel.

রদজওয়াব, A. *n.* Rejoinder, reply.

রদ্দী, A. *adj.* Waste, rejected.

রপ্তানী, P. *n.* Export.

রপ্তে রপ্তে, P. *adv.* Gradually, slowly.

রফা, A. *n.* Settlement of a dispute; compromise.

রফা করা, A. *v.* To settle, to dispose of.

রফানামা, A. *n.* An award; a written deed of settlement; a deed of compromise.

রফাদফা, A. *adj.* Settled, decided.

রফীক, A. *n.* A companion, a friend; an adherent.

রফু, A. *n.* A darn.

রফু করা, A. *v.* To darn.

রফুগর, A. *n.* A darner.

রফুগরী, A. *n.* Darning.

রব, A. *n.* Lord, God.

রবাব, A. *n.* A stringed instrument.

রবী, A. *n.* Spring. The third and fourth months of the Muhammadan year. as রবী-আল্-আও-উল্, the third month, or first *Rabi*; রবী-উস্-সানী, the third month or second *Rabi*.

রব্বানী, A. *adj.* Divine.

রমজান, A. *n.* *Ramadhan*, the ninth month of the Muhammadan year. The name of the fast celebrated in the month *Ramadhan*.

রয়ীস, A. *n.* A chief, a prince, a leader; a citizen.

রয়ুব, A. *n.* Fear.

রশওয়ৎ—*See* রেশ্ওয়ৎ.

রশীদ, A. *n.* A guide, a director.

রসদ, P. *n.* Imports; grain, provisions, rations.

রসম—*See* রস্ম.

রসমী, A. *adj.* Usual, customary.

রসান, P. A suffix denoting bearing, bringing, giving.

রসীদ, P. *n.* A receipt, an acknowledgment.

রস্ম, A. *n.* Toll, duty; fees, postage.

রসুল, A. *n.* A messenger, a prophet; one who has been given a Book or dispensation. A *Nabi* may have neither, and is therefore considered of a lower class.

রহন, A. *n.* A pawn, a mortgage, a pledge, security for a loan.

রহন রাখা, A. *v.* To pledge, to mortgage.

রহনদার, A. *n.* A mortgagee.

রহননামা, A. *n.* A deed of mortgage.

রহীন, A. *adj.* Pledged.

রহানী, A. *adj.* Pertaining to a mortgage.

রহানী খৎ, A deed of mortgage.

রহ্ন, A. *n.* Mercy.

রহম করা, A. *v.* To have mercy, to feel compassion.

রহমৎ, A. *n.* Mercy, compassion.

রহমান, A. *adj.* Merciful ; আল্-রহমান, The Merciful (God.)

রহীম, A. *adj.* Merciful, compassionate. (Muslim commentators of the Quran affirm that রহমান should only be used of God, whereas রহীম may be used of both God and man.)

রাই—*See* রায়.

রাইয়ৎ, A. *n.* A subject, a tenant ; a farmer.

রাইয়ৎনামা, A. *n.* A written engagement given by a farmer to his landlord.

রাইয়তী, A. *n.* Tenantry. *adj.* Pertaining to a farmer or tenant.

রাইয়তী পাট্টা, a lease given to a cultivator.

রাইয়তী জমী, lands the rent of which is paid in money.

রাইজ, A. *adj.* Customary, usual, current.

রাইস—*See* রয়ীস.

রাওয়ী, A. *n.* A narrator. (Sometimes written রাবী.)

রাকিম, A. *n.* A writer ; a correspondent.

রাজ, P. *n.* A mason, a bricklayer. (Properly a *head mistri.*)

রাজী, A. *n.* Pleasure, satisfaction, acquiescence. *adj.* Contented, satisfied ; agreed, willing.

রাজীনামা, A. *n.* A deed of acquittance ; a document certifying the approval of anyone, a deed of consent.

রাজেক, A. *n.* Provider ; one of the names of God.

রাড়, H. *n.* Dispute, quarrel, war.

রাণ, P. *n.* The thigh.

রাতিব, A. *n.* A daily ration.

রাতিবা, A. *n.* Salary, allowance, pension.

রাতিবাখোর, A. *n.* A pensioner.

রাফদী, A. *n.* A heretic.

রাবিতা, A. *n.* Relation, connection, union.

রাবী—*See* রাওয়ী.

রায়, A. *n.* Judgment, verdict.

রায় দেওয়া, A. *v.* To give a verdict, to pass judgment.

রায় বাহাদুর, A title of honour.

রায় সাহেব, A title of honour.

রাস্ত, P. *adj.* Right, proper, true.

রাস্তগু, P. *adj.* Truthful.

রাস্তবাজ, P. *adj.* Honest, upright.

রাস্তবাজী, P. *n.* Honesty, integrity.

রাস্তা, (P. রাস্তহ্). *n.* A road, a way.

রাস্তী, P. *n.* Truth ; uprightness, honesty.

রাহৎ, A. *n.* Ease, peace, repose.

রাহনুমা, P. *n.* A guide, a pilot.

রাহনুমাই, P. *n.* Guidance.

রাহা, (P. রাহ). *n.* A road, a way.

রাহাগীর, P. *n.* A traveller.

রাহাজান, P. *n.* A highwayman, a robber.

রাহাজানী, P. *n.* Highway robbery.

রাহী, P. *n.* A traveller, a wayfarer.

রাহেন—*See* রহন.

রাহেব, A. *n.* A monk, a hermit.

রিওয়াজ,—*See* রওয়াজ

রিওয়ায়ৎ, A. *n.* A tale, a narrative, a tradition. (In Islam the word is technically used for a tradition beginning with the words 'It is related,' and having nc *isnad* or chain of relators).

রিকাব—*See* রেকাব.

রিজক A. *n.* Daily food ; an allowance.

রিজামন্দ—*See* রজামন্দ.

রিজাল, A. *n.* Men.

রিফু,—*See* রফু.

রিয়া, A. *n.* Hypocrisy.

রিয়াকার, A. *n.* A hypocrite.

রিয়াসৎ, A. *n.* Nobility, greatness ; lordship, authority.

রিসালা, A. *n.* A pamphlet, a treatise ; a letter ; a mission, a message ; a troop of horse.

রিসালাদার, A. *n.* The commander of a troop of horse.

রিসালাদারী, A. *n.* The occupation of a *risaladar.*

রুকন, A. *n.* A pillar, a prop ; the essential part of anything.

রুকু, A. *n.* Bowing the body in prayer, genuflection ; a section of the Quran marked by a *ruku.* (See further under রকাৎ.)

রুখ্সৎ, A. *n.* Leave, permission ; dismissal.

রুখ্সৎ হওয়া, A. *v.* To take leave, to depart.

রুজু, (A. রুজুয়). *n.* A returning, a confronting ; inclination ; a reference ; an appeal. *adj.* Filed, presented, referred to.

রুজু করা. A. *v.* To file, to institute, to bring to court, to lay before.

রুজু রুজু, A. *adv.* Face to face.

রুজু মুকাবেলা, A. *n.* Presence ; a confronting.

রুপোশ, P. *adj.* Absent, concealed.

রুপোশ হওয়া, P. *v.* To abscond.

রুমাল, (P. রূমাল). *n.* A handkerchief, a towel.

রুসওয়ারী, P. *n.* Infamy, disgrace.

রুসুল, A. *n.* Prophets. (*Plu.* of রসুল.)

রুইয়ৎ, A. *n.* View, aspect ; countenance.

রুইদাদ, A. *n.* A statement, a record.

রুবকার, P. *n.* An order. *adj.* Eager, zealous.

রুবকারী, P. *n.* A judicial proceeding, a record in a case ; a requisition.

রুবকারী হওয়া, P. *v.* To be tried (a case).

রুবরু, P. *adv.* Face to face ; in the presence of.

রুবাই, A. *n.* A metrical stanza of four lines.

রুয়াক—*See* রওয়াক.

রুম, A. *n.* Turkey. (The word was originally used of the Eastern Roman Empire).

রুহ, A. *n.* Spirit, soul ; breath ; wind.

রুহানী, A. *adj.* Spiritual.

রেওয়া, P. *n.* Balance-sheet ; statement of receipt and expenditure.

রেওয়াজ, A. *n.* Custom, practice, habit ; currency, prevalence.

রেওয়াজী, A. *adj.* Current, usual.
রেওয়ায়ৎ—*See* রিওয়ায়ৎ.
রেকাৎ—*See* রকাৎ.
রেকাব, A. *n.* A stirrup.
রেকাবী, A. *n.* A dish; a copper plate.
রেখ্তা, P. *n.* A kind of verse; mortar *adj.* Mixed.
রেজ্কী, (P. রেজগী). *n.* A fragment, a fraction; small change.
রেজা, P. *n.* A scrap, a particle; a mason's labourer.
রেজাই, P. *n.* A bed-quilt; a wrapper.
রেয়াজ—*See* রেওয়াজ.
রেয়ায়ৎ, A. *n.* Kindness, favour; remission. (Also written রেয়াৎ.)
রেয়ায়ৎ করা, A. *v.* To forgive, to excuse.
রেশ্ওয়ৎ, A. *n.* A bribe, an illegal gratification.
রেশ্ওয়ৎ দেওয়া, A. *v.* To bribe.
রেশ্ওয়তী, A. *n.* One who takes bribes.
রেশ্ওয়ৎখোর, A. *n.* One who takes bribes.
রেশতা, P. *n.* Relation, connection, alliance.
রেশতাদার, P. *n.* A relation, a relative.
রেশম, P. *n.* Silk.
রেশমী, P. *adj.* Silken.
রেসালা—*See* রিসালা.
রেহন—*See* রহন.
রেহাই, P. *n.* Exemption, escape, discharge, freedom, release.
রেহাই দেওয়া, P. *v.* To release, to discharge, to set free.
রেহেম, A. *n.* The womb.
রোকড়, H. *n.* A cash-book; a day-book.
রোকা, H. *n.* A call, a shout.
রোক্কা, A. *n.* A letter, a note.
রোখ, P. *n.* Face; aspect, side.
রোখ্সৎ—*See* রুখ্সৎ.
রোজ, P. *n.* A day: daily wages; *adv.* Daily.
রোজ্-কিয়ামৎ, the Day of Ressurrection.
রোজ্ রোজ্, P. *adv.* Daily, day by day.
রোজ্গার, P. *n.* Service, employment, livelihood; earnings, means of subsistence.
রোজ্গার করা, P. *v.* To earn: to start in business.
রোজ্গারিয়া, P. *adj.* Working for hire; earning.
রোজ্নামা, P. *n.* A diary, a journal, a day-book.
রোজ্বরোজ, P. *adj.* Day after day.
রোজা, P. *n.* A fast. The thirty days fast in the month *Ramadhan.*
রোজাদার, P. *n.* One who observes the fast.
রোজানা, P. *adj.* Daily: daily wages.
রোজী, P. *n.* Daily allowance, maintenance.
রোজীনা, P. *n.* Daily allowance or wages.
রোল করা, *n.* Whipping (in tailoring).
রৌজা, A. *n.* A garden, a shrine.
রৌনক, A. *n.* Colour; splendour; dignity. *adj.* Brilliant, splendid.

রোশন, P. *n.* Bright, luminous, shining.

রোশনী, P. *n.* Light, illumination.

রোশনী করা, P. *v.* To lighten, to illuminate.

রোশন-চৌকী, P. *n.* A band of musicians.

ল

লওয়াজিম, A. *n.* Necessaries; perquisites; effects.

লওয়াজিমা, A. *n.* Zemindari documents.

লকড়ী, H. *n.* Wood; a staff, a stick.

লকব, A. *n.* A title; a surname.

লগাম, P. *n.* A bridle.

লগায়েৎ—*See* লাগায়েৎ.

লঙ্গর, P. *n.* An anchor; a thick cable; a piece of cloth worn round the waist.

লঙ্গর করা, P. *v.* To cast anchor.

লজ্জৎ, A. *n.* Taste, flavour, enjoyment.

লড়কা. H. *n.* A son; a boy.

লড়কী. H. *n.* A daughter; a girl.

লড়াই. H. *n.* Contention, quarrel; war.

লৎকান, A. *v.* To hang, to suspend.

লতফ,—*See* লুতফ.

লতীফ, A. *adj.* Subtle, rare; light.

লতীফাহ্, A. *n.* A witticism; *latifa.*

লফজ, A. *n.* A word; a saying.

লফজী, A. *adj.* Verbal, literal, textual.

লবাদা, P. *n.* A cloak.

লবান—*See* লোবান.

লয়ন, A. *n.* A curse. (Also written লান).

লয়নৎ—*See* লানৎ.

লম্বাদার, P. *n.* One who pays rent to Government in the name of several others.

লশ্‌কর, P. *n.* An army; a sailor: a soldier, a *lascar.*

লশ্‌করী, P. *n.* The profession of a soldier or sailor. *adj.* Belonging to the army.

লহ্‌জা, A. *n.* Tone, accent; moment, instant.

লহু, H. *n.* Blood.

লহু-জারী, H. *n.* A flow of blood, an issue of blood.

লা, A. A negative particle corresponding with the English in, un, non, &c. as লা-ওয়ারিস. heirless; no, net.

লাও—*See* নাও.

লা-ওয়ারিস, A. *adj.* Heirless.

লা-ওয়ারিস করা, A. *v.* To disinherit.

লাকিন, A. *con.* But, yet.

লাখরাজ, (A. লা-খিরাজ) *adj.* (Land) free of rent. [free land.

লাখরাজদার, A. *n.* A holder of rent-

লাগাম--*See* লগাম.

লাগায়েৎ, A. *prep.* Until, till, up to; inclusive: to the end.

লাঙ্গর—*See* লঙ্গর.

লাচার, P. *adj.* Helpless, hopeless.

লাচারী, P. *n.* Helplessness.

লাজ, H. *n.* Shame.

লা-জওয়াব, A. *adj.* Speechless, having no reply.

লাজেম, A. *adj.* Compulsory, necessary, incumbent upon.

লান, (A. লয়ন). *n.* A curse, an imprecation.

লানৎ, A. *n.* A curse, an imprecation.

লায়্‌ল্‌, A. *n.* Night.

লায়লৎ-উল্‌-কদর. the night of power, when the Quran is said to have descended from heaven.

লায়েক, A. *adj.* Worthy, capable, fit.

লায়েক হওয়া, A. *v.* To deserve, to be worthy of : to suit.

লাল, P. *adj.* Red.

লালচ, H. *n.* Covetousness, greed.

লাশ, T. *n.* A dead body. a corpse.

লা-শক, A. *adv.* Doubtless. without doubt.

লা-শরীক. A. *adj.* Without a partner. (Said with regard to God's unity.)

লিবাস, A. *n.* Clothes.

লিয়াকৎ, A. *n.* Worth, ability, skill, fitness.

লিয়াকতী, A. *adj.* Worthy. skilful.

লিসান, A. *n.* The tongue : a language.

লিহাজ, A. *n.* Notice ; deference ; reference, relation : shame.

লিহাজ করা. A. *v.* To take notice of, to pay respect to, to be partial to.

লুগাৎ, A. *n.* A dictionary.

লুচ্চা, H. *n.* A scamp, a libertine. *adj.* Lewd, lascivious.

লুচ্চানী, H. *n.* Libertinism, corruption, rascality.

লুতফ, A. *n.* Taste, pleasure ; elegance.

লূমড়ী. H. *n.* A fox.

লৈকিন—*See* ল্যাকিন.

লেংড়া, H. *adj.* Lame.

লেফাফা, P. *n.* A cover. an envelope.

লোকসান—*See* নোকসান.

লোণ্ডা, H. *n.* A slave ; a boy

লোণ্ডী, H. *n.* A female slave ; a girl.

লোন, H. *n.* Salt.

লোনা, H. *adj.* Saltish, brackish.

লোন্তা, H. *n.* Saltness.

লোবান, A. *n* Frankincense.

লোবানদানী. A. *n.* A censer for incense.

লৌহ. A. *n.* A plank. a board ; a tablet ; a title-page.

লৌহ মহফুজ, the tablet on which the Quran is said to have been written in heaven.

শ

শওয়াল,—*See* শোয়াল.

শক. A. *n.* Doubt, suspicion. (See further under শোক.)

শক্ত, (P. সখত). *adj.* Hard, severe, difficult, strict, unfeeling.

শকল, A *n.* Form, shape.

শখস, A. *n.* A person, a man.

শতরঞ্জ, P. *n.* Chess. A carpet.

শতরঞ্জবাজ, P. *n* A chess-player.

শতরঞ্জী, P. *n.* A carpet.

শদীদ, A. *adj.* Strong, violent, severe.

শফকৎ, A. *n.* Kindness, affection.

শফা, A *n.* Healing, curing.

শফা করা, A. *v.* To heal.

শফায়ৎ, A. *n.* Intercession, mediation.

শফায়ৎ করা, A. *v.* To intercede.

শব, P. *n.* Night.

শব-ই-বরাৎ, the fourteenth night of the month *Shaban* in which God is said to write down the actions of men for the coming year; the Muslim festival held on that occasion, which consists of prayers, illuminations etc.

শব-ই-কদর, A night in the month Ramadhan, in which the Quran is said to have been sent down to earth.

শম্শীর, P. *n.* A sword.

শমস, A. *n.* The sun.

শমসী, A. *adj.* Solar.

শয়তান, A. *n.* Satan.

শয়তানী, A. *adj.* Satanic. *n.* Wickedness, evil.

শয়র. A. *n.* Poetry; a couplet.

শরক, A. *n.* The East; the rising of the sun.

শরকী, A. *adj.* Eastern. Oriental.

শরৎ, A. *n.* A stipulation, condition, agreement. (Also written শর্ত.)

শরৎ রাখা, A. *v.* To wager.

শরতী, A. *adj.* Conformable to.

শর্বৎ, A. *n.* A decoction of sugar and water, *sherbet.*

শরম, P. *n.* Shame, modesty.

শরমিন্দগী, P. *n.* Shamefacedness.

শরমিন্দা, P. *adj.* Ashamed, bashful, modest.

শরফ. A. *n.* Precedence, honour, dignity.

শরফরাজ, A. *adj.* Exalted. distinguished.

শরফরাজী, A. *n.* Distinction. dignity.

শরা A. *n.* Muhammadan ecclesiastical law: the *sharia.* (Often written শরে.)

শরয়ী. A. *adj.* Legal, lawful, in accordance with Muhammadan ecclesiastical law.

শরহ, A. *n.* Explanation, commentary; rate (of assessment), charge.

শরাব. A. *n.* Wine, spirits.

শরাবখোর, A. *n.* A drunkard.

শরাবী, A. *adj.* Intoxicated, *n* A wine bibber, a drunkard.

শরারৎ, A. *n.* Wickedness, villany.

শরীক, A. *n.* A partner. a sharer. a confederate.

শরীকী, A *adj.* Belonging to more than one person, joint. *n.* Partnership.

শরীফ, A. *adj.* Noble, high, sacred. *n.* The ruler of Mecca, the *Shareef.*

শরীফৎ, A. *n.* Nobility, rank.

শরীফা, A. *n.* The custard-apple.

শরীর, A. *adj.* Wicked, evil.

শরীয়ৎ, A. *n.* Muhammadan ecclesiastical law.

শরীয়তী, A *adj.* Legal; in accordance with ecclesiastical law.

শর্ত—*See* শরৎ.

শহওয়ৎ, A *n.* Lust.

শহওয়ৎ করা, A. *v.* To lust after.

শহওয়ৎপরস্ত, A. *adj.* Lustful, sensual.

শহদ, P. *n.* Honey.

শহর, P. *n.* A city, a town.

শহরৎ—*See* শোহরৎ.

শহাদৎ, A. *n.* Testimony, martyrdom.

শহীদ, A. *n.* A martyr. a witness.

শাই, A. *n* A thing, a subject.

শাগরদ, (P. শাগিরদ). *n.* A disciple, a pupil.

শাতের, A. *adj.* Smart, clever.

শাদা—*See* সাদা.

শাদী, P. *n.* A marriage ; pleasure.

শাদীয়াৎ, P. *n.* Fees paid for marriages.

শাদীয়ানা, P. *n.* Marriage fees or presents made by peasants to the zemindar.

শান, A. *n.* Condition ; eminence, glory ; sheen, lustre.

শান নজুল, the conditions and circumstances under which a certain revelation is made.

শাদী সেলামী, P. *n.* Same as শাদীয়ানা.

শানক—*See* সহনক.

শাফী, A. *n.* *Al Shafi* the founder of one of the Muslim schools of jurisprudence.

শাফে, A *n.* An intercessor, a mediator.

শাবান, A. *n.* The name of the eighth month of the Muhammadan year.

শাবাশ, P. *int.* Well done ! bravo !

শাবাশী, P. *n.* Encouragement, applause.

শাম, P. *n.* Evening.

শাম্লা (A. শমলহ). *n.* A kind of pugaree.

শামা (A. শমআ). *n.* A lamp, a candle.

শামাদান, A. *n.* A candle-stick.

শামিয়ানা, P. *n.* An awning, a canopy as *shamiana*.

শামিল, A. *adj.* Comprising. including ; united or added to ; connected with. *Prep.* With, along with.

শামিল করা, A. *v.* To join. to connect ; to affix, to append : to include.

শায়াতীন, A. *n.* Satans. (*Plu.* of সয়তান.)

শায়ের, A. *n.* A poet.

শায়েস্তা, P. *adj.* Proper, right ; polite, meek.

শায়েস্তগী, P. *n.* Fitness ; politeness.

শারহ, A. *n.* A commentator. an exegete.

শাল, P. *n.* A shawl.

শালগম, P. *n.* A turnip.

শালিস—*See* সালিস.

শাহ, P. *n.* A king, a *shah.*

শাহজাদা, P. *n.* A prince.

শাহজাদী, P. *n.* A princess.

শাহাদৎ—*See* শহাদৎ.

শাহিদ, A. *n.* A witness.

শাহিদী, A. *n.* Attestation. witness, testimony.

শিকদার, P. *n.* A Muhammadan officer formerly appointed to collect land revenue. Now a Muhammadan patronymic.

শিকদারী, P. *n.* The occupation of a *shikdar.*

শিকম, P. *n.* The womb, the abdomen.

শিকমী, P. *adj.* Private, secret : dependent, subordinate.

শিকমী প্রজা, P. *n.* A sub-tenant.
শিকরা, P. *n.* A hawk.
শিকস্ত, P. *n.* A breach, a fracture; loss. damage. defect.
শিকস্তা, P. *adj.* Broken: defeated. শিকস্তা জমী. lands broken away by the river.
শিকায়েৎ, A. *n.* Complaint, accusation, defamation.
শিকার, P. *n.* Hunting: game.
শিকার করা, P. *n.* To hunt.
শিকারী, P. *n.* A hunter.
শিজরা, A. *n.* A genealogical table.
শিতাব. P. *adv.* Quickly, directly.
শিতাবী, P. *n.* Haste, speed.
শিদ্দৎ, A. *n.* Severity, violence, strength.
শিন্নি, (P. শীরীণী). *n.* Sweetmeats: an offering of sweetmeats etc., made in the name of God or some saint at the fulfilment of a vow, or on some religious festival. (Sometimes written ছিন্নি.)
শিরক. A. *n.* Polytheism: the ascribing partners to God (Sometimes written শেরেক.)
শিরাকৎ, A. *n.* Partnership, combination: a company.
শিরিশ—*See* সিরীশ.
শীয়া, A. *n.* A sect: the Shiah sect of Muhammadans.
শীরীণ. P. *adj.* Sweet.
শীরীণী. P. *n.* Sweetmeats.
শীশী, P. *n.* A phial, a small glass bottle.
শুকর, A. *n.* Thanks, gratitude; praise.
শুকর করা. A. *v.* To thank, to express gratitude.
শুকরগুজার, A. *adj.* Thankful.
শুকরগুজারী, A. *v.* Thanksgiving.
শুকরাণা. A. *n* Thanksgiving. a thank-offering.
শুগল. A. *n.* Work. occupation, employment.
শুজায়ৎ, A. *n.* Bravery, courage.
শুতর, P. *n.* A camel.
শুবা. A. *n.* Doubt. uncertainty: flaw.
শুবা করা. A. *v.* To suspect, to doubt.
শুমার, P. *n.* Calculation, number. estimate, account, reckon.
শুমার করা, P. *v.* To number, to reckon.
শুমারী. P. *n.* Enumeration.
আদম শুমারী, Census.
শুরু, A. *n.* A beginning.
শুরু করা. A. *v.* To begin, to lead the way: to establish.
শুর্বা. P. *n.* Broth, soup.
শেখ, A. *n.* An old man: a chief; one of the four classes into which Indian Muslims are divided.
শেগাফ. P. *n.* A split, a crack.
শেতাব—*See* শিতাব.
শেনাখৎ, P. *n.* Recognition, identification. (Often written শেনাক্ত.)
শেনাখৎ করা, P. *v.* To recognise; to identify.
শেয়ানা—*See* সেয়ানা.
শের, P. *n.* A lion.
শেরেক—*See* শিরক.
শোয়াল, A. *n.* The month *Shawwal*, the tenth of the Muhammadan year.

সায়েল, A. *n.* A beggar ; a questioner ; a petitioner, an applicant.

সায়া, P. *n.* A skirt, a petticoat.

সারা, H. *adj.* All, whole.

সারাকালী, H. *n.* Superficial area.

সারেং, (P. সরহঙ্গ). *n.* A chief, a captain of a ship ; a *serang.*

সাল, P. *n.* A year.

সাল তমামী, A. *n.* Annual accounts.

সালানা, P. *adj.* Annual, yearly. *n.* An annual pension ; lands taken for one year only. (Sometimes written সালিয়ানা.)

সালানাদার, P. *n.* An annuitant, a pensioner.

সালাম, (A. সলাম). *n.* Salutation ; blessing ; peace, security. *Int.* Good-bye ! farewell ! good-day !

সালাম আলাইকুম, Peace be upon you ! (The orthodox Muslim greeting).

সালামৎ, A. *n.* Peace, security ; protection.

সালামী, A. *n.* A fee paid by a tenant as cash down when leasing land. (See further under শাদী.)

সালী, A. *adj.* Autumnal ; land on which autumnal crops are grown.

সালিক, A. *n.* A traveller ; a term used by Sufi mystics to describe a stage in spiritual progress.

সালিম, A. *adj.* Safe, whole.

সালিস, A. *n.* An arbitrator, a referee, an umpire, a mediator.

সালিসনামা, A. *n.* An arbitration award.

সালিসী, A. *n.* Mediation, arbitration ; award. *adj.* Mediatory.

সালিসী করা, A. *v.* To mediate, to arbitrate.

সালিসী-ইকরারনামা, A. *n.* A written agreement to abide by the award of an arbitrator.

সাহাবা, A. *n.* Friends, companions, owners. (*plu.* of সাহেব.)

সাহেব, A. *n.* A companion, a friend ; a lord, a master ; Sir ; a European ; *Esp.* a title of distinction given to the personal disciples of Muhammad.

সাহেবা, A. *n.* Lady, madam. (*Fem.* of *saheb*)

সাহেবানা, A. *n.* The behaviour of a *saheb.*

সাহেবী, A. *n.* Pertaining to a *saheb*, European.

সিওয়া, A. *prep.* Except, besides.

সিক্কা, A. *n.* A coin ; a rupee ; a stamp, a seal, an impression on money.

সিক্কাজান, A. *n.* A coiner.

সিক্কাজানী, A. *n.* Coining.

সিজদা—*See* সেজদা.

সিজিল, A. *n.* A register, a decree of a judge ; a written attestation before a notary. *adj.* Prop well-arranged.

সিজিল করা, A. *n.* To arrange.

সিতার, P. *n.* A guitar with three strings.

সিতারবাজ, P. *n.* One who plays on the *sitar.*

সিতারা, A. *n.* A star ; fate, destiny.

সিতুন, P. *n.* A pillar, a column.

সিদক, A. *n.* The truth.

সিদ্দিক, A. *n.* True, veracious.

সেরেস্তা, (P. সেরেশতা). *n.* An office, employment ; a record, a register : connection, affinity ; usage, custom.

সেরেস্তাদার, P. *n.* An office-holder ; a record-keeper, a *serestadar*, the superintendent of a court office.

সেলা—*See* সিলাহ্.

সেলাম—*See* সালাম.

সেহর, A. *n.* Magic, enchantment.

সেহা, (P. সেয়াহা). *n.* An entry of payment of rent in a zemindar's account-book.

সেহা করা, P. *v.* To write an entry of payment of rent in an account-book.

সেহা-নবীস, P. *n.* One who keeps a zemindar's account-books.

সেহা-বহি, P. *n.* The book in which a zemindar's entries of rent paid are kept.

সৈয়দ, A. *n.* A lord, a chief : a title of the lineal descendants of Muhammad ; one of the four classes into which Indian Muslims are divided.

সোব্হান—*See* সুব্হান.

সোলে—*See* সলাহ্.

সোহরৎ—*See* শোহরৎ.

সৌগাৎ, T. *n.* A present.

সৌগন্দ, P. *n.* An oath.

সৌদা, P. *n.* Goods, merchandise ; trade.

সৌদাগর, P. *n.* A merchant, a trader.

সৌদাগরী, P. *n.* Trade. commerce ; the business of a merchant.

সৌদাগরী করা, P. *v.* To trade.

সৌদা-পত্র, P. *n.* A bill of sale ; a written agreement to sell on certain terms.

স্ফূর্তি, (A. ফর ?). *n.* Haste, quickness, energy.

স্ফূর্তি করা. A. *v.* To hasten. to move with alacrity.

হ

হওয়া. A. *n.* Air, wind ; flight ; climate.

হওয়াই, A. *n.* A sky-rocket ; fireworks.

হওয়ালদার, P. *n.* A native subordinate military officer.

হওয়ালা, A. *n.* Commitment, charge, custody : reference, allusion.

হওয়ালা করা. A. *v.* To make over, to give in charge, to surrender, to deposit.

হওয়াস, A. *n.* The senses.

হওলাৎ, (A. হওয়ালাৎ) *n.* A lock-up ; a deposit, a loan especially which does not carry interest. (Sometimes written হাওলাৎ).

হওলাৎ করা, A. *v.* To put in custody ; to take a loan.

হক, A. *n.* Truth, justice. *adj.* True right ; just.

হক চকান, A. *v.* To be confused.

হকদার, A. *n.* The holder of any right ; a proprietor ; a recipient.

হকদারী, A. *n.* Proprietorship.

হক সফা, A. *n.* Right of pre-emption.

হক নাহক, A. *adv.* Rightly or wrongly.

হকবা—*See* হক্‌বা.

হকীকৎ, A. *n.* Truth, sincerity; right, title: an account, a narrative.

হকীকী, A. *adj.* Real, true, genuine.

হকীম, A. *n.* A doctor, a physician: *Esp.* one who practices medicine according to Arab methods.

হকীমী, A. *adj.* Medical.

হকীয়ৎ, A. *n.* Proprietorship: rights.

হকীর, A. *adj.* Contemptible, despicable.

হকুক, A. *n.* Rights, interests: privilege.

হকানী, A. *adj.* Divine.

হগা, H. *v.* To ease oneself (Often written and pronounced হাগা.)

হজ, A. *n.* Pilgrimage to Mecca.

হজ করা, A. *n.* To go on pilgrimage to Mecca.

হজম, A. *n.* Digestion; embezzlement.

হজমী, A. *adj.* Promoting digestion.

হজর, A. *n.* A stone; hindrance, prohibition.

হজরৎ, A. *n.* A title of respect; your highness, your worship.

হজামৎ, A. *n.* Shaving, cupping; robbery.

হজিব নোকসান, A. *n.* A partial exclusion from inheritance.

হজ্জাম, A. *n.* A barber, a cupper.

হতিয়ার, H. An instrument; a weapon.

হডডী, H. *n.* A bone.

হদীস, A. *n.* A tradition. (See further under হুরং.)

হদ্দ, A. *n.* A boundary, a limit; the maximum.

হদ্দজওয়াব, A. *n.* The reply in legal proceedings.

হদ্দতলব, A. *n.* The total due to anyone.

হদ্দবন্দী, A. *n.* The settlement and demarcation of boundaries.

সরহদ্দ, boundary, limits, frontiers.

চৌহদ্দ, limits, boundaries.

বে-হদ্দ, boundless, unlimited.

হদীয়া, A. *n.* A present, a gift.

হফতা, P. *n.* A week: Saturday.

হবশী, A. *n.* An Abyssinian.

হবস, A. *n.* Imprisonment, confinement.

হবীব, A. *adj.* Beloved. *n.* A lover, a friend.

হম, P. A prefix used in compounds to signify sameness or connection: also, like, fellow, co.

হম-জিনস of the same kind, homogeneous.

হম-পেশা, a fellow-tradesman.

হম-রাহী, a fellow-traveller.

হমদ, A. *n.* Praise.

আল্ হমদ, the opening words of the first chapter of the Quran. and so one of the names eiven to that chapter.

হমল, A. *n.* A load, a burden.

হমলা, A. *n.* Assault, attack. stroke.

হমায়েল, A. *n.* A small Quran, often suspended from the neck as a charm.

হমীদ, A. *adj.* Praised; praise-worthy.

হমেশা, P. *adv.* Always. incessantly. (Often written হামেশা.)

হায়া, (A. হয়া). *n.* Shame, modesty. বে-হায়া, shameless.

হায়াৎ—*See* হয়াৎ.

হায়বৎ, A. *n.* Awe, horror.

হারাম, (A. হরাম). *adj.* Unlawful, forbidden.

হারামজাদা, A. *n.* A term of abuse, as scoundrel ; bastard.

হাল, A. *n.* State, condition ; present time. *adj.* Present, current, as হাল সন, the current year. হাল-খাতা, a current account : a new account opened at the beginning of a new year.

হাল্কা—*See* হলকা.

হালৎ A. *n.* State, condition, circumstances ; nature.

হালাক,—*See* হলাক.

হালাল, (A হলাল). *adj.* Lawful, permitted.

হালাল করা, A. *v.* To kill an animal for food according to Muslim rites.

হালী, A. *adj.* Present, current ; new, fresh.

হালেফ, A. *n.* One who takes an oath.

হাশিয়া, A. *n.* A border, a hem ; a marginal note.

হাসিল, A. *n.* Revenue ; produce : profit, gain. *adj* Complete, full.

হাসিল করা A. *v.* To gain, to obtain, to realise to collect

হাসিলা, A. *adj.* Cultivated, arable.

হিকমৎ, A. *n.* Knowledge, skill, wisdom.

হিকমতী, A. *adj.* Wise, skilful.

হিকারৎ, A. *n.* Contempt, scorn.

হিজরা, A. *n.* The flight of Muhammad from Mecca to Medina in 622. A.D. ; the era reckoned from that date : emigration. (Also written হিজরী and হিজরৎ.)

হিজারৎ—Same as হিজরা.

হিফজ করা, A. *v.* To commit to memory.

হিফাজৎ, A. *n.* Custody, protection, care.

হিফাজৎ করা, A. *v.* To preserve, to guard.

হিফাজৎখানা, A. *n.* A record room.

হিবা, A. *n.* A gift.

হিবানামা, A. *n.* A deed of gift.

হিমাকৎ, A. *n.* Folly, stupidity.

হিমায়েৎ, A. *n.* Protection, guardianship, patronage.

হিমায়েৎ করা, A. *v.* To espouse one's cause ; to protect.

হিয়াজৎ, A. *n.* Joint acquisition.

হিম্মৎ, A. *n.* Courage, spirit, enterprise.

হিম্মতী, A. *adj.* Courageous, spirited.

হিরজ, A. *n.* Custody.

হিরস, A. *n.* Greed, covetousness.

হিরাসৎ, A. *n.* Custody, charge, care.

হিস্‌সা, A. *n.* A share, a portion.

হিস্‌সাদার, A. *n.* A sharer, a partner ; a shareholder.

হিস্‌সাদারী, A. *n.* Partnership.

হিসাব, A. *n.* Account, reckoning ; rate.

হিসাব করা, A. *n.* To count, to calculate.

হিসাব দেওয়া, A. *v.* To render an account.

হিসাবদিহি, A. *n.* Responsibility.

হিসাবনিকাশ, A. *n.* A written statement of credit and loss.

হিসাবরক্ষক, A. *n.* An accountant.

হিসাবী, A. *adj.* Calculating, prudent.

হিসাবনবীস, A. *n.* An accountant.

হীলা, A. *n.* Fraud, deceit.

হীলাবাজ, A. *adj.* Deceitful.

হুকবা, A. *n.* A long period of time; eighty years.

হুকুম, A. *n.* An order, a command; award. [order.

হুকুম করা, A. *v.* To command, to

হুকুমতামিল, A. *adj.* Obedient.

হুকুমদার, A. *n.* An orderly.

হুকুমনামা, A. *n.* A written order; a warrant.

হুকুমবরদার A. *adj.* Obedient.

হুকুমৎ, A. *n.* Government, sovereignty, administration.

হুজরা A. *n.* A cell; a private room.

হুজুগ, A. *n.* A hoax; a false rumour.

হুজুগে, A. *adj.* One fond of idle tales.

হুজুর, A. *n.* Presence. *Int.* Your honour! Sir!

হুজুরী মহল, A. *n.* An estate paying revenue direct to Government.

হুজুরী তালুক—Same as হুজুরী মহল.

হুজ্জৎ, A. *n.* An altercation, a dispute; a proof: persistence.

হুজ্জতী, A. *adj.* Disputatious, obstinate, argumentative. *n.* A wrangler, a disputant.

হুণ্ডি, H. *n.* A bill of exchange.

হুদা, A. *n.* Guidance, revelation.

হুনর, P. *n.* Cleverness, dexterity, skill.

হুনরী, P. *adj.* Clever, dexterous.

হুরমৎ, A. *n.* Chastity, honour, dignity.

হুরমতী, A. *adj.* Chaste: having dignity.

হুরমৎ-দাবী, A. *n.* Claim for damages for libel.

হুরূফ, A. *n.* The letters of the alphabet.

হুলইয়াহ, A. *n.* Countenance: description of a person.

হুলইয়াহনামা, A. *n.* A written description of an absconding criminal.

হুশ, P. *n.* Sense; understanding.

হুশইয়ার, P. *adj.* Sensible, intelligent.

হুশইয়ারী, P. *n.* Sensibleness, intelligence.

হুশমন্দ, P. *adj.* Sensible.

বে-হুশ, P. *adj.* Senseless.

হুসন, A. *n.* Beauty, goodness.

হুর, A. *n.* The virgins promised to Muslims in Paradise.

হেদায়ৎ, A. *n.* Guidance; precept.

হেদায়ৎ করা, A. *v.* To guide, to direct.

হেরফৎ, A. *n.* Trade, profession: skill, art. (Also written হেরফা)

হেরফতী, A. *adj.* Cunning, clever.

হেরেম—*See* হরম.

হেয়েস—*See* হিরস.

হৈকল—*See* হয়কল.

হোকবা—*See* হুকবা.

হৌজ, A. *n.* A reservoir, a pond.

হৌল, A. *n.* Terror, dread, fear.

হৌলনাক, A. *adj.* Dreadful.